HIGH TIMES
presents

Paul Krassner's

Pot Stories
for the Soul

foreword by Harlan Ellison

Stories by and about Ken Kesey, Stephen Gaskin, Allen Ginsberg,
Michelle Phillips, Abbie Hoffman, Mountain Girl, Jerry Rubin,
Hunter S. Thompson, Stan Mack, Wavy Gravy, Lynn Phillips, Robert
Anton Wilson, Harry Shearer, Kate Coleman, John Sinclair, Jack
Herer, David Peel, Pot Star, Michael Simmons, Mark Mothersbaugh,
Jonathan Pekar, and many, many more.

Produced by Steven Hager & L.E. Vans
Editor: Paul Krassner
Art Director: Frank Max
Managing Editor: Zena Tsarfin
Production: Robert Braswell & Devin Horwitz
Cover Painting: Mark Arminski

First edition: October 1999

ISBN#: 1-893010-02-3

This book is dedicated to Peter McWilliams, whose creative and compassionate leadership in the medical marijuana movement has continued to be inspiring and invigorating.

Other books by the author:

Confessions of a Raving, Unconfined Nut: Misadventures in the Counter-Culture

The Winner of the Slow Bicycle Race: The Satirical Writings of Paul Krassner

Impolite Interviews

Table Of Contents
Family Ties by Stan Mack
Foreword by Harlan Ellison
Introduction by Paul Krassner

STAN MACK'S REAL LIFE FUNNIES

ALL DIALOGUE GUARANTEED OVERHEARD

YOU
HEAD.

HAVE
E MY
OU GO ON.
CK UP.

I JUST REMEMBERED, I HAVE TO CALL ANDREA, YOU GO AHEAD, I'LL LOCK UP.

FINE

BUT I HAVE TO USE THE BATHROOM, SO YOU GO ON...

OKAY, SEE YOU IN THE MORNING.

I HAVE
AND
Y, YET.

RIGHT!!
EAVING!!
ODBYE!!

LAM

=PUFF, PUFF= I CAN'T WAIT TO GET BACK TO SCHOOL WHERE I DON'T HAVE TO HIDE MY POT SMOKING FROM MOM.

=PUFF, PUFF= I CAN'T WAIT FOR HIM TO GO BACK TO COLLEGE SO I CAN SMOKE A JOINT IN MY OWN APARTMENT.

SERVICE

T'anks But No T'okes
Foreword
by Harlan Ellison

Basically, fuck dope. No offense, dude, but: fuck dope. This has virtually nothing to do with the subject at hand, but as deep background permit me this brief preamble: I ran away from home at age 13. I'd already been earning my living for three or four years prior to that, apart from mooching off my parents in Painesville, Ohio.

I mean, I was 9 or 10, fer chrissakes, so when I say "I was earning my own living" I mean I was paying for everything a kid of 9 or 10 in the early Forties would need money for: 10 cents admission every Saturday afternoon to the Lake Theater, the latest issue of Big Shot Comics featuring Skyman and Tony Trent as The Face, an occasional Grosset & Dunlap hardcover of a Lone Ranger novel ($2 each) bylined by Fran Striker, who had created the radio show and the character, but actually ghostwritten by the unsung Gaylord DuBois, a new pair of US Keds hightops with the big red ball on the side, a Tom Mix "nuclear bombardment chamber" radio premium ring for 10 cents and two Ralston Purina box tops, a bottle of Teel tooth drops, some Fleer's Double Bubble...I earned the money for such staples by selling the Sunday edition of the *Cleveland Plain Dealer* every Saturday night at the corner of State and Main Streets, by shining shoes at that same excellent location, by mowing lawns raking leaves shoveling snow catching flies cleaning garages and attics. Back in the days before the discovery of Cultural Guilt and the advent of the Victim Society, that was how us lower-middle-class white boys paid our way. It was a hardscrabble existence for Clark Bars.

And then I ran away. And began to earn my keep for real. No mommy bargaining that if I'd eat my peas and carrots I could stay up an hour later to hear *Big Town* or *The Hermit's Cave*. No father saying if I cleaned my room, I could come downtown after he closed the store on Saturday night and we'd have hot roast beef sandwiches and french fries at Jerry & Bert's. It was *La Strada*, dude. I was on the road, sans bucks, sans mommy/daddy, sans even Kerouac—who wouldn't be published yet for another decade. I worked farms and orchards, picking crops. I bluffed my way into truck-driving jobs on construction sites. I worked in a lumber camp, on tuna boats, as a door-to-door salesman, short order cook, printer's devil and slag-bucket carrier in a lithographing plant, garbage collector. I worked in a carnival, on a road gang, in a quarry, standing by the side of the road selling bouquets of flowers. I lied to farmers' wives and told them I could repair the busted washing machine (or mangle, or stove, or hot plate) out there rusting in the side yard, in exchange for a meal. I rode the rods, I drank gypsy coffee out of a tin can with Princes of the Road under railroad trestles in 10 different states, I had my ass saved a hundred times by men of many other colors, and I was locked up in the old Kansas City slam with a carny geek who had gone "wetbrain" so long ago that the scent of rancid sour mash came out of his pores when he sweated.

I saw what liquor and dope had to offer. I have been around drugs all my life. I came back with Chinese food one night, to a sleazy railroad flat I was sharing with a beautiful girl, and found her dead, naked, OD in the tub. The water was still warm. I actually heard Charlie Parker blow, one night, at a $1 admission rent and spaghetti party up on a hundred and first and First Avenue in Harlem; and he went into the can, went Charlie "Bird" Parker, and he fixed, and he came out, and he blew...crap. Discordant shit. I heard the great legend Bird blow, only that once, a year or two before he died, and he sounded like shit. From the dope.

Here is the subject at hand: I have been on the street since I was 13. I have learned important stuff about staying alive. I have learned that sneaky bastards and kindhearted slobs come in all colors. I have learned that you're never as smart as you think you are. I have learned that love is rare but cowardice is plentiful. I believe that anything not nailed down is mine—and anything I can pry loose ain't nailed down.

All through the Sixties and Seventies, going to parties and just hanging, this one or that one would offer me a hit of this or a lid of that. Drop one of these, stick this in your instep, shove this spansule up your ass, honk a line of this, inhale a vape of this...I always said, no thanks.

I wasn't afraid. Ask anyone who knows me. I don't scare. Simply put, I didn't want any part of that crap. When someone would thrust a doobie the size of a Macanudo under my nose and intone the magic word, "Toke?" I'd reply, with a sweet smile, "Not till I come down." Theodore Sturgeon (if you don't recognize the name, go look it up, you ignorant asshole) once wrote that he'd seen studies of people who allegedly produced psilocybin in the bloodstream. He opined that I was like that...always high. Otherwise, how to explain all the weird stuff I've done in my life?

The subject at hand is Krassner asking me to write my "dope story" for his idiot book.

Here it is.

Fuck dope.

Oh, and....Have a nice day.

III • Pot Stories For The Soul

Introduction
by Paul Krassner

The priorities are insane. Cigarettes are legal and kill 1,200 people a day—in this country alone—but marijuana is illegal and the worst that can happen is maybe you'll raid your neighbor's refrigerator.

When former drug czar William Bennett was asked about the number of deaths caused by marijuana, the only example he could come up with was a Canadian railroad-train engineer who had apparently been smoking pot before an accident he caused. I mention this not to trivialize the deaths of those who lost their lives in that train wreck, nor of those who died in a more recent accident caused by a marijuana-smoking bus driver, but Bennett is cruel to exploit those tragedies in order to justify arresting anyone, as Lenny Bruce said, "for smoking flowers." There have been more than 12 million marijuana busts in America since 1965, and that injustice is the unspoken underbelly of every anecdote in *Pot Stories For the Soul*.

Indeed, as former *High Times* editor Peter Gorman told reporters at the magazine's 10th annual Cannabis Cup in Amsterdam: "While we would never dismiss or diminish the suffering of any group at the hands of another—and if we could stop their suffering somehow, I hope that we would have the courage to work towards that end—there are in fact several hundred million marijuana and hashish smokers worldwide being prosecuted, jailed and sometimes put to death in more than one hundred separate countries simply for their use of cannabis. There is no other group, no religious organization, no single kind or color of people who are persecuted in such numbers in so many different places anywhere on the globe.

"Which does not diminish the suffering of anyone. It is not a contest. Certainly the threat of being sentenced to a year in jail in the US or France or England does not compare to the threat of marauders killing everyone in a village simply for having religious beliefs. But neither should your persecution go unnoticed. And it is precisely because there are so many of us being threatened, beaten, jailed, losing our property and denied our rights, so many of us who are suffering for our belief in this gentle and healing herb that we have become the single largest persecuted minority on the planet."

I don't care that Bill Clinton was the recipient of several blow jobs from Monica Lewinsky in the Oval Office; I'm more concerned that the president has advocated the requirement of a drug test before an individual is allowed a driver's license. One can almost hear Mr. Rogers' friendly voice asking, "Can you say fascism?" And Clinton is opposed to medical marijuana. "I feel your pain," he is saying. "I just don't want to help relieve it." When sitcom cancer patient Murphy Brown smoked medical marijuana to relieve her chemotherapy-induced nausea, Thomas Constantine, head of the Drug Enforcement Administration, announced that he was checking to see "if any laws were broken." Well, not the First Amendment, anyway.

Back in real life (speaking of the First Amendment), an anti-drug booklet with a foreword by Senator Orrin Hatch informs parents that among the warning signs their children are using marijuana or other drugs is "excessive preoccupation with social causes, race relations, environmental issues, etc." In Mississippi, anyone found guilty of possessing marijuana for any reason could face the removal of a limb if proposed legislation became law. Rep. Bobby Moak (R.-Lincoln County) introduced a bill which authorized "the removal of a body part in lieu of other sentences imposed by the court for violations of the Controlled Substances Law." Keith Stroup, executive director of the National Organization for the Reform of Marijuana Laws, called the measure "political posturing at its most extreme. This is a truly barbaric proposal that shocks the conscience." A provision in the bill mandated that a convicted person and the court "must agree on which body part shall be removed."

It's no longer enough that folks have to decide whether to support Scientology or the German government; whether to carry their groceries in paper or plastic ("Just say hemp"); whether to believe Bill Clinton or Paula Jones. Now you also have to choose between sacrificing an arm or a leg. And even that seems humane in comparison to former House Speaker Newt Gingrich's sponsorship of federal bill HR 41, which would require the death penalty for individuals convicted of importing illegal drugs into the United States—including marijuana. Capital punishment could conceivably apply to someone who imported more than fifty grams of pot. That's less than two ounces. Curiously, back in 1982, Gingrich wrote a passionate letter to the Journal of the American Medical Association attacking the "outdated federal prohibition" of medical marijuana. He decried the plight of "thousands of glaucoma and cancer patients" held hostage by "bureaucratic indifference."

The good news is that voters in six states and Washington, DC have voted for medical-marijuana initiatives (Arizona and California did so in order to emphasize that they really meant it when they voted for medical marijuana in the previous election). The bad news is that the federal government is ignoring the mandate of the people. States' rights—it's not just for racists anymore. Peter McWilliams, Los Angeles author of *Ain't Nobody's Business If You Do: The Absurdity of Consensual Crime*, has AIDS and cancer. He needs to smoke marijuana in order to counteract nausea. If he throws up, the pills he takes to stay alive are regurgitated along with his lunch. The DEA has arrested him as the ringleader of a conspiracy to cultivate and distribute medical marijuana. This is the drug-war equivalent to the Chicago Conspiracy Trial of protesters against the Vietnam War.

But the tide continues to turn. In Boston, 45,000 people rallied to support the legalization of marijuana. One pop-cultural sign of a changing climate was the movie *Half Baked*, a sort of *Dumb and Dumber* for potheads, cowritten by and starring stand-up comic Dave Chappelle. John Brodie wrote in the February 1998 issue of *Details* magazine:

"*Half Baked*'s journey from Chappelle's head to theatrical release shows that weed—after a 15-year absence wrought by Nancy Reagan and the timidity of studio execs—may no longer be anathema in Hollywood. Tommy Chong believes a cultural shift is already at hand. 'I could not even get a meeting during the Reagan years,' he says. 'One of the reasons that Cheech and I broke up is that Universal offered him a movie without me, based on the fact that it wouldn't be a pot movie. That was *Born in East L.A.*'

"Chong, who is bullish enough on pot comedies to be self-financing his own, *Tommy Chong's Best Buds*, maintains that things are about to change because a silent stoner majority, who do not subscribe to the 'pot will rot your brain' theory, have come of age, and those kids who grew up watching his movies are now in positions of power in Hollywood. 'There are,' he says in a conspiratorial tone which suggests he may be keeping a list, 'potheads in charge of the studios and the networks.'"

Chappelle, in the process of promoting *Half Baked*, was a guest on the *Late Show with David Letterman*. When Letterman asked him outright if he smoked marijuana, Chapelle hesitated, milking the silent tension. Then he said, "Yes," pausing for effect, and added, "but only for medicinal purposes." Laughter and applause ensued, but that joke was a truism, according to the gospel of

Dennis Peron, co-author of Proposition 215, who has stated seriously that "All marijuana use is medicinal."

I began collecting the material in *Pot Stories For the Soul* a year ago by writing to 250 friends and acquaintances, requesting their accounts of experiences with marijuana. Then I put announcements in my satirical newsletter, *The Realist*, in my *High Times* column, "Brain Damage Control," in a *Funny Times* article, in a *Factsheet Five* ad, on Roy of Hollywood's midnight show on KPFK and on Bob Fass' midnight show on WBAI in New York.

Incidentally, there will be only six more issues of *The Realist* before it ceases publication. If you'd like to subscribe, send $12 to Box 1230, Venice CA 90294. And be sure to ask for your free tube of Y2KY Jelly to ease your transition into the 21st Century.

The stories in *Pot Stories For the Soul* were chosen because they're funny, whimsical, bizarre, poignant and, yeah, soulful, you got a problem with that? The styles may be different, but all are revealing snippets of an essentially good-natured subculture. A typical correspondent, Louise Calabro, wrote, "I'm sure that I have some funny dope stories, but I can't remember any." Another, Chip Gatzert, confessed, "I expanded my mind so many times, I've got stretch marks on my brain."

I am now collecting material for a sequel, *Acid Trips For the Soul*, so please send me your LSD (or other psychedelic) story at the address two paragraphs up or e-mail me at pkrassner@earthlink.net and, if I include it in the book, you won't be identified unless you wish, and you'll receive a free copy when it's published, so be sure to include your snail-mail address.

And, the next time you see anti-marijuana propaganda from the Partnership for a Drug Free America, remember that legal drug pushers have a vested interest in keeping illegal drugs unpopular, as indicated by the sponsors of that organization. The following statistics have most likely risen since the time period they cover, 1988-91: The Partnership received $150,000 each from Philip Morris (Miller beer and Marlboro cigarettes), Anheuser-Busch (Budweiser) and R.J. Reynolds (Camel). Other contributors: American Brands (Jim Beam and Lucky Strike), Pepsico and Coca-Cola. Contributing pharmaceutical companies included Bristol-Myers Squibb, CIBA-Geigy, Dow, DuPont, Glaxo, Hoffman-LaRoche, Johnson & Johnson, Merck, Pfizer, Schering-Plough, Smith-Kline and Warner-Lambert. Publishing companies Time-Warner, Dow Jones and Reader's Digest also contributed funds.

As long as the government can arbitrarily decide which substances are legal and which are illegal, then those who remain behind bars for illegal substances are political prisoners. And Kenneth Starr's perversion of prosecutorial power is what goes on every day in the war on drugs.

Significantly, unlike dangerous and addictive drugs such as alcohol or tobacco, marijuana is sold solely on the basis of word-of-mouth. That's the purest form of advertising, and it's free. Currently, over 10 million Americans enjoy smoking marijuana. So, all together now, let us chant: "We don't need no steenkin' Joe Camel!"

May, 1999
Venice Beach, California

Chapter I

Countercultural History

Turning On *Newsweek*
Kate Coleman

I just love it when people in high places quit their jobs and then expose the fancy people they used to work for. I devoured every word penned by Jackie Kennedy's former secretary, Mary Gallagher, when she disclosed to the world her boss' finicky demands to have her nylons hand-ironed after laundering, and her penchant for selling her hardly-worn clothes to discreet second-hand shops rather than giving them to her maids the way most rich women do. Ex-establishment people have a real fascination for me. I myself am one of them, and this is my exposé. I worked for three years at *Newsweek*, half a block from St. Patrick's Cathedral. I quit the magazine in October 1968 and fled the country for a year to regain my sanity.

I came to *Newsweek* after 5-1/2 years at the University of California at Berkeley, armed with a B.A. sloppily attained in English and a political education and lifestyle carefully nurtured through years of demonstrating, organizing, arguing, turning on and free loving. I had been busted once, for ecstatically sitting in as a fanatical adherent of the Free Speech Movement. My sentence was a light one, due to the recommendation of my probation officer. She was favorably impressed with me for no other reason than liking a CBS documentary on the FSM, entitled *The Berkeley Rebel*, in which I had appeared. I was the archetype of the Berkeley liberated woman and, like Joan of Arc, I cut off all my long, black hair and headed for the big city and the real world to act out my destiny. In this state, I fell upon *Newsweek*.

For the full three years I was at the magazine, I was always startled by people's reactions to my working there. Old politico friends from Berkeley whom I would see from time to time looked askance at me and mumbled under their breath that I had sold out. Maybe my Berkeley friends were right. From the Free Speech Movement to *Newsweek*?

Was I or was I not co-opted? At *Newsweek* I was the house Freako-Doper-Lefty and I was tolerated, later even indulged, because I carefully cultivated the illusion that I knew everything about drugs and which buildings would be taken over next at which school. Men and women alike at *Newsweek* cultivated a knowing air of sophistication about everything in the world. After all, the magazine touched on everything in the world within its covers. They prided themselves on their "hip" ability to assimilate anything that might take place—as long as the impact was first tempered by being filtered through *Newsweek*.

For the first eight months I was a "clipper," brandishing my "rip-stick" (a yard-long piece of metal with a single-edged razor on one side) at eleven newspapers a day, searching for stories for the Nation department to rewrite at the end of the week. Omigod, every day clipping out pieces of newsprint and filing them in little cubbyholes for writers who worked wedged into coffin-sized cubicles—and all the while congratulating myself for having landed a glamorous New York job, out-competing 500 other identically-qualified liberal arts, Betty Co-ed graduates. I can't tell you how thrilling it was to work in such an important place. I took home $65 a week for the privilege and was even supplied with a khaki uniform smock denoting my status. Ostensibly, the smock was utilitarian rather than an indication of caste, to save the clippers' clothes from newsprint smudge. In my case, however, it hid the fact that I had to wear the same clothes every day because my salary only permitted such luxuries as toilet paper and lunch.

When I was hired, there was no such thing as a male clipper. Later, the whole system was altered and girls were hired directly as researchers. Clippers were hired on a permanent basis and did not have to have a college degree. But during my early employment, I developed a hatred of all the young hotshots coming out of Harvard and other Ivy League holes who held degrees identical to mine, but who, because of their penises, were automatically sent to one of the bureaus and paid $120 a week to become writer-reporter trainees.

But besides career promises, there was a wonderful lack of formality about the place that belied the stigma of my drab smock. Everyone was on a first-name basis. I could call editor Osborn Elliott "Oz." Writers would talk to me and call me by my first name. Very early in my clipper days, I established myself as an authority on hippies, drug addicts and leftists. And it was smoking dope that got me my first reporting assignment, liberating me from the clip desk. It was unheard of for a clipper to do reporting, but I had a special background.

The Nation department was doing a story on the scene in Greenwich Village—drugs, runaways, lifestyles. Despite the fact that they had New York-based reporters and some half-dozen researchers sitting there, Senior Editor John Jay Iselin (a 36-year-old, short, dark-haired man who always appeared in shirtsleeves and wore suspenders) decided to make use of the magazine's Berkeley freak for an undercover assignment. I dressed up like a hippie and hung out on McDougal Street and in Washington Square, asking teenagers from Queens if they turned on or fucked. While there, I met a very hip and talkative dealer, went to his apartment, interviewed him and bought a tiny chunk of hash which I duly brought into Iselin's office the following morning to show him. He peeled back the tinfoil as delicately as a demolition expert, asking all kinds of dumb questions about how you smoke it, what the high was like and if it was addicting. When I told him I'd had to buy it so that my dealer friend would trust me, he instructed me to fill out an expense account form. Did he want the hash? "Oh, no," he said quickly. "You keep it."

"How do I write it up," I asked naively—"$15 for hashish?" (I had never filled out an expense account form before.)

"Put it down as entertainment," said the great-great-great-great-grandchild of America's first chief justice.

In the summer of 1967, *Newsweek* indirectly bought enough grass and paraphernalia to warrant a felony sentence in New York of from one to 15 years. Only three years behind the times, it was decided to do a cover story on marijuana, and, naturally, I was assigned to the story. The cover designer, Bob Engels, uncertain of what he wanted, allowed me to hunt up paraphernalia and other material for a cover photo. I went down to the Lower East Side's Psychedelicatessen and purchased two beautiful water pipes, a hash pipe, roach holders, a dozen packets of cigarette papers and a few little psychedelic toys. What a haul! I also bought two ounces of Acapulco Gold and one ounce of Panama Red from my favorite exclusive downtown dealer. *Newsweek* footed the whole bill without a ripple, and I got the payola of a lifetime. But it didn't end there. The fact that marijuana was to be legitimized twixt the pages of *Newsweek* gave rise to unexpected curiosity on the parts of both the senior editor and the writer of the piece, both of whom decided, independent of each other, that their respective editing and writing would lack verisimilitude unless they tried the stuff. The writer, Paul Zimmerman, was a graduate of Amherst with a masters from Berkeley, a chubby, dark-haired, easygoing fellow in his early 30s who was quickly ascending the *Newsweek* hierarchy. He played it safe and took the dope and my instructions home with him to share with his wife. Liking it, he nevertheless castrated his story, balancing the viewpoint to be exactly in the wishy-washy middle—even before he was edited.

Ed Diamond, the 45-year-old senior editor, wanted atmosphere as well as dope. He asked me in conspiratorial tones if he couldn't come down to my place to try it out. For a moment I was panicked, as my past proselytizing for the weed included my testimony that it enhanced lovemaking. But I was mistaken in my fears, for he quickly added that he would like me to invite some of my pot-smoking friends. And so I invited some of my more respectable dope-smoking, ex-Berkeley friends to be good Samaritans to my boss. Frantically, I cleaned my West Village apartment, borrowed chairs and colored lights from the gay man next door, and bought all kinds of head food to delight the palate of the stoned. On the afternoon before the engagement, Diamond called me into his office. He looked worried. Uh, he paused, would...uh...I mind if...uh, his wife, Adelina, came too? Ed had compulsively confessed what he was doing, and his suburbanite wife insisted on coming. I didn't mind at all. The family that smokes together goes on to better things. Ed and my friends came on schedule; the wife came later. I had the best of all possible dope rolled and set out on the table. We all began smoking and conversing in awkward tones. The senior editor, however, didn't know how to inhale (shades of Bill Clinton), as he was not a smoker, thus necessitating the use of special paraphernalia to insure his getting high. Adelina, quiet and withdrawn, smoked and smoked and never said a word, but later sat there with a weird smile on her drawn face. Ed conversed as energetically as he would at any cocktail party, while my friends and I got so high our tongues stuck to the roofs of our mouths. The rest of us had had enough, but Ed wouldn't smoke unless we continued, so we kept on going. I staggered into the kitchen to prepare the goodies and was swept by a tidal wave of dizziness. Blackness encroached along the edges of my vision, and I realized with horror that I was about to pass out—I had OD'd in my zeal to get that maniac high. I lurched through the living room. "Heh...heh...ha, ha...I...uh...hmmmm, ah...smoked a little too much hash...don't...uh...judge by me...be with y'all in a sec...." I lay down on my bed and listened to the screaming silence from the next room. "I blew it," I thought. I recovered shortly and fed them, but Diamond wouldn't smoke any more, and he and his wife soon left, thanking me profusely for a wonderful time. Later, he told me his wife had loved the stuff, but that he only got a slight "buzz." I made a vow never to play guru again.

After the cover story came out with the only piece of actual writing I was ever allowed to do for the magazine—it was so heavily edited that all statements which seemed to emanate from my own personal knowledge of grass were deleted and substituted with phony quotes from people who didn't exist; Oz was fearful lest Newsweek readers get the idea that a staffer smoked the stuff with the magazine's approval—I was approached by people all over the magazine, asking me to get them some pot. They all wanted to try it, but were afraid of buying it from some shady dealer. Me they trusted, and for a week I toyed with the idea of increasing my meager earnings by being Newsweek's exclusive dealer, but in the end I decided I didn't want to deal with the notorious suspiciousness of novice smokers who see any dealer as someone who's out to burn them. And they were so straight, too. During the marijuana issue, I came to work with some Japanese incense and lit it in the office I shared with Zimmerman. The smell went all the way down the drab, institutional corridors, prompting editors and researchers to come banging on my door to verify their suspicions that, at last, they had smelled the sinister weed. Amazing. They not only had never smelled pot, they didn't even know what incense was. I was ordered to stop burning the stuff.

To be fair, I wasn't the only one at *Newsweek* who had ever turned on. A few of the researchers had occasionally imbibed, but only one of them could be classified as a head, and she was circumspect about it. I was pleased that one ex-Harvard writer whom I initiated became a confirmed head. It led, I am convinced, to his leaving *Newsweek* and eventually heading for hip San Francisco and a television job.

One late Friday night, while a blizzard raged outside, he and I sat in my office with the window wide open and the snow pouring in, furtively puffing away at three joints in a row, giggling hysterically and half hoping we would be discovered. I am sad to say it was the only time that I turned on at work. It was my choice; I could have done it easily enough. But I hated the sterility of the place. The walls were the same color as my discarded clipper's smock, and the lights were naked fluorescent fixtures. Only the senior editors on up rated a carpet and a colored wall. To prevent retina regurgitation, I bought rose-colored glasses for my myopic eyes and plastered my side of the office walls with offensive collages of LBJ, Vietnam atrocities, naked balling couples and Fillmore art-nouveau posters. Zimmerman's side of the room was bare, and he bitched to me that he didn't want to have to look at napalmed babies every day when he worked. Other visitors also complained that my choice of wall art was tasteless and offensive, but I was the self-appointed scourge of *Newsweek* and believed it was good for them. When I appeared on a CBS network documentary on marijuana, urging viewers to turn on, CBS disguised my identity by saying I worked for an unnamed major magazine and left it at that, so *Newsweek* didn't care.

Excerpted from an article in *Scanlan's*.

Love and Haight
Lynn Phillips

When I graduated Radcliffe without having met a Harvard man who could support me in the style to which my mother, a lawyer, had always aspired, she took me shopping and made me try on mink coats. Obviously I would need a disguise if I was to attract the right sort of victim. I put on a few to humor her and hated every one of them passionately. I wanted to look like I'd been dragged through a gutter by a herd of wild horses, not like I'd been insulated from the vicissitudes of life by a roster of ranch minks. It's important to remember that at this point in subcultural history it was hard to hate mink coats generically. No one was referring to fur coats as "dead animals" or spraying them with red paint. So if you didn't want a mink, you had to hate them one by one. As I did so, sneering at each one's hemline, color and cut, my mother concluded that my attitude was too immature for real mink—so she bought me a *starter mink*.

It was the cheapest kind in stock—a black, dyed Japanese mink. It had a stand-up collar, raglan sleeves, and it tied at the waist with a thin leather belt which was a good deal softer than the fur itself. I don't know what they feed minks in Japan, something perhaps grown in the ruins of Hiroshima, but whatever it is makes their hair quite strong. Almost wiry. The words "mink coat" evoke a luxuriant sensuality, but, I noted with a certain bemused fascination, my mink was more like a body-sized beard. I resolved to wear it with irony. No sooner was I wrapped in its folds than I began to choreograph my escape from everything my mother hoped it would drag me into. My first move was to visit my friend, Judy, who had dropped out of college to live with an artist on the Haight. It was 1967, and the Haight was what it called "happenin'." Judy's artist boyfriend had stopped painting and turned into a jeweler. Obediently, so had Judy.

They lived behind their little silver shop literally on Haight Street just a puff or two from Ashbury. I got to sleep on a foam rectangle on the floor in the back of their flat like a derelict—my lifelong dream. And sleeping, I soon realized, was all I wanted to do, because to step outside onto Haight at that time was utterly and profoundly exhausting.

Mario Savio, the leader of the Free Speech rebellion that spawned the Love Generation, and the Diggers who worked the dumpsters and donors to feed it, were brilliant, industrious visionaries. They organized more positive human energy with less autocratic nonsense than any of us have seen before or since. The Haight was Anarchism's last and best stand—a triumph of the human spirit, at least for the many who had some.

Inspired by the visible showmen who grabbed the media and ran—first away with it and then into its arms—a second tier of strong personalities flowed into whatever vacuums of responsibility arose. They certainly weren't in it for the money, and they weren't there to etch their names into history—the era is remembered for its marketable bell-bottoms, not for its remarkable success in refuting the need for top-down authority—but they came forward and did what needed doing for no reward other than the expression of their own generosity, hope and style.

They wrangled with cops, overdoses, health problems, kids' animal needs and questions of justice. They put out newspapers, organized clothing exchanges, ran a small subsidiary economy based on recycling and drugs. They worked, and worked hard.

Equally numerous, however, were the sheep. "Express yourself. Be an individual. Do your thing, man. Don't be conformist. I'm an Aquarian. Have another toke." These banal and ulterior words, or words so like them as to be dismally indistinguishable from them, gushed from the river of drug-crazed ersatz pirates, hobos, clowns, Edwardian decadents and Peruvian peasants burbling down the pavement. A chick could not get to the corner to score a pack of cigarettes without a proposition of some kind. And she was obliged, style-bound, to look happy to get it, whether it was an offer for Meth, or Reds, or a toss on the mat with someone who would soon evolve into either Charlie Manson or a 12-stepping bore.

Hey, Mamma: How about a groovy group grope in a purple-painted hovel? How about a chance to cook rice with some beautiful, blond, big-breasted beauties in tiny tie-dyed T-shirts while we guys drive up the coast to hammer nails into redwoods so we can fuck up the clear-cutters' bandsaws? Sounds ab-so-fucking-lutely like wow, but, uh, maybe later. Too many choices make me drowsy, man.

Judy and her boyfriend rapidly perceived that I had no desire to leave my foam, and he didn't like that. I was a bad influence, meaning, I think, that when I was napping in the cubicle next door Judy felt constrained about making noises in bed. Because she loved me and didn't want to hurt my feelings by asking me to leave, they conspired to fix me up for the weekend to get me out of there.

The man with whom I was to journey was named Steve. He was from Connecticut, which Mother would have approved, but he drove a Norton, which, I was assured, was the coolest fucking motorcycle in the world. I crammed my starter mink into my little duffel bag, jumped on & behind him and held on for the ride.

I don't remember where we went. Today, Judy said that she

thinks it was Stinson Beach. Something like that. Anyway, Steve had a friend who was doing some construction work on a house sitting on stilts overlooking the Pacific, and we could stay there while construction was in progress. I don't remember seeing any construction, and I don't remember ever seeing the ocean. Either it was wrapped in mist, as often happens, or we were too stoned to distinguish ocean from sky.

What I do remember is that the pot was free, and plentiful, and that Steve and I did not have a very good time. I wanted him to find some reason to adore me. I didn't care what reason that was, nor could I think of any suggestions offhand, but that was all I wanted, and I was decidedly not getting it. I did my best to fake an orgasm, which was what one did back then to be adorable, but Steve, ahead of his time, wasn't buying.

"I want to see your clit twitch," he explained patiently. "If it doesn't, it means that you aren't really coming." I considered this piece of intelligence with more credulity than I subsequently learned it deserved. I was still young enough to believe that there was something fun about my body left to learn. A little more dope, I figured, might help.

That set the pattern for the weekend. I desired; he refused; he demanded the implausible; I had another toke; and repeat. Eventually he wandered off down the hill to watch Nature's clit twitch, leaving me on my cot with a copy of *Macbeth*.

I read it for what seemed like days. I was in the mood by then for the Shakespearean tool-kit of storms and power and witches and murder. The words bounced around in my head, glowing, rolling down ravines of marijuana and drifting up, burning off the page like fog rising up over the California hills. "Words to the heat of deeds too cold breath gives"? Puzzling and divine as California itself.

The next morning, still stoned, we headed back. A storm gathered up around us and the air turned cold. I put on my Japanese mink with a dirty olive poncho over it tied with electrical cord so that Steve wouldn't fixate on what a Bergdorf Goodman Bohemian I was. It rained abruptly and dramatically (*The Tempest* came to mind), and then it was over. As the clouds swept away, a siren sounded.

Steve pulled over, and we got off the Norton, stoned and nervous. As if under orders from my mother, I removed my poncho to reveal my starter mink and my "good upbringing."

The cop swaggered over at a leisurely pace.

"We saw you throw that bottle away," said the cop to Steve, which was interesting, because I hadn't noticed a thing.

The co-cop, who had gone snooping off to the side of the road, returned with an amber pill-bottle with crud in it. He opened it.

"It's full of roaches," he said.

"I guess we're going to have to take you in," the first cop gloat-
ed.

This was my chance to escape my fate. A jail term on a drug rap,
even a trumped-up one, would take me out of the Misfit Class and
catapult me all the way into Instant Hipness. I was envisioning
myself in jail, strip-searched nightly by giant matrons, ripening
slowing into a female Genet, when I noticed the two cops
bundling Steve into their car and preparing to drive away.

"Hey," I actually said, "what about me?"

Cop number one explained that I wasn't under arrest. He agreed
to take me in so that I could get a ride back to Judy's from the station. But to do that we had to wait for a separate car and a
matron. He waited with me.

On the way back, I asked the cop if he'd read any good books
lately. He said that he was enjoying *Exodus*. Because he knew that I
was from Jew York, as it was known in those parts, and that Steve's
name was Levy, I understood that he was reassuring me that he, at
least, was only interested in persecuting Steve for his taste in
drugs, not his ethnic origin.

I encouraged him to deliver his synopsis of the plot, hating
myself for feigning an interest in airport literature simply to flatter
a tyrant. But I did strenuously recommend *Macbeth*.

Turned out that the place Steve had been arrested in was
Redwood City. I didn't know at the time that it was one of the
most conservative, hippie-hostile places on the West Coast, but as I
sat in the molded plastic chair in the Redwood City Police Station, I
started to worry about what would happen if Steve was actually
jailed.

He could easily get five years for those joints. And I'd feel obliged to visit him in prison. I'd have to stay in California, learn to
drive, and give up my entire life out of loyalty to this cool guy who
didn't even like me, and who I wasn't all that crazy about, either.

At that point, just as my stomach was doubling its knot, a pair
of cops entered, Stage Right, with a German Shepherd. They started giving it orders in German.

"Alt!" one exclaimed.

The dog sat.

"Achtung!" shouted the second new cop.

I clutched my rough mink to my cheek as if it was something
Audrey Hepburn might want to be buried in, whipped out my
trusty *Macbeth*, and tried to look both genteel and Gentile.

"Your dogs speak German," I observed graciously. "Is it because
they were trained there?"

"We use German commands so that ordinary people can't order them around," lied the larger cop with the sort of smile a Nazi would use to lure you to the "showers."

After a very long time, during which I reread *Macbeth* with equally little comprehension and far less pleasure than before, the co-cop emerged from a "secure area" and asked if I was the girl who had been with Levy. I said I was, and waited for the oppressor's ax.

"I hope your friend didn't pay money for that pot of his," said the cop dryly, "because according to the lab, if he did, he was had."

He took a kind of snickering pleasure, I felt, in eviscerating any delusions of Hipness I might have had left. The upshot was, they hit Steve up for a zillion parking tickets. Friends came to bail him out, and by nightfall I was back on my foam pallet at Judy's, dampening her love life.

Afterwards, I imagined that my mink had savèd Steve as well as me. I never really enjoyed reading Shakespeare before or since, so I knew our dope was good. Therefore, I surmised, it had to be pity for lovely, classy, minky me that had persuaded the Gestapo to let him off. It didn't occur to me until years later that he may have traded in his dealer for his freedom. I'll never know what exactly happened, because I didn't see Steve again after that. I learned a few years later that he had drowned in shallow water while helping someone move a boat. He may have hit his head on a rock, Judy thought. The details were officially confusing. Later I wondered if perhaps a dealer he'd ratted on had gotten out of jail and done him. I'll never know, like I said. But it was thanks to what happened that day with him that I finally understood the Great American Truth that my mother, the lawyer, was trying to impart to me personally, and it is this: The bad news is that, try as you might to move up or dive down, you will never escape your class. The weird news is that, no matter what your class is, no matter whose skin you're wearing or what you're smoking, there are fleeting moments in the vicissitudes of life when this bad news will save your hide.

Chapter 2

The Kesey Papers

The Bust at Kesey's Place
Lee Quarnstrom

Exhausted by several days of Prankster foolishness that we were calling "space travel," I was napping one evening in a back bedroom of Ken Kesey's cabin in the forested mountains above Palo Alto on the San Francisco Peninsula, when I heard Michael Hagen's voice shouting something about a search warrant. Search warrant? We'd been expecting something like this, but I was in no mood to stick around to see what this search-warrant business was all about. It sounded like Hagen was out front somewhere, so naturally I was up and heading out back. I was halfway to the door in the back bedroom before I was even awake.

As I dashed into the darkness of the back bedroom, someone tossed me the mayonnaise jar with all the pot in it. Expecting a raid, we'd consolidated all the dope into one quart jar so it could be more easily disposed of in an emergency such as the one we were now apparently encountering.

The jar was about two-thirds full. It was enough for two or three days.

I scrambled across a bed and started out the door, hoping to hustle the few yards down to the edge of La Honda Creek and, under cover of the total darkness you find at night in a redwood forest, toss the stash as far as I could into the stream. Hopefully, I was thinking as I stumbled toward the door, the mayo jar would smash on one of the boulders in the creek and the evidence would be washed away westward to the Pacific, a few miles down La Honda Road.

The trouble was, as I scooted out the door I ran straight into the barrel of an automatic pistol that was pointed directly at my forehead! I could feel the gun at the bridge of my nose. It was cold! It was hard! It was scary!

"Stop or I'll shoot," the gunman shouted, displaying no originality, I thought as I turned.

Foolheartedly, I didn't believe he'd actually shoot me over something as benign as a little illegal weed, so I ran back into the room. The cop, probably as confused and scared as I, stumbled into the blackness behind me. He grabbed my ankle as I started to crawl back across the bed, the mayonnaise jar still in my hand. Realizing that the room was pitch black, I understood in that instant that he'd never be able to recognize me in the light.

On the other hand, of course, he could have shot me! So I kicked him in the chest and tried to break loose. Another Prankster, Hagen I think, dashed into the bedroom headed toward the door into the bathroom—which had two entrances, the other off the kitchen. I lobbed the mayo jar to Hagen and followed him into the john.

What a sight! There was Kesey, who'd been dabbing yet another touch of Day-Glo paint to the constantly expanding mural-montage that covered the walls, the porcelain and every other surface of the bathroom. Only now he was busy with the more pressing business of flushing the grass down the toilet. The Best Foods jar was empty! At the same moment, a fat Asian man who turned out to be the late federal drug agent, Willie Wong, ran into the bathroom from the kitchen, smacked Kesey's balding head with a huge flashlight, then jumped onto his back.

Now, Kesey had been a championship wrestler during his college days at the University of Oregon. He was strong, agile and, just then, operating on adrenaline. He stood up from the swirling toilet bowl, agent Wong clinging to him. With a terrific shrug, Kesey tossed him from his back onto Page Browning, a.k.a. Des Prado, who was standing frozen at the sink where he had been shaving. Somehow, despite the chaos going on around him, Page was still applying the razor to his skinny face.

Wong, still armed with the huge Ray-O-Vac, landed on Page like a sumo wrestler as he was tossed from Kesey's back. The pair of them, Wong and Page, tumbled into the bathtub.

Page still held the razor in his hand. Suddenly the bathroom window was shattered by a huge automatic pistol that extended into the room.

"Stop or I'll shoot," the gunman shouted from outside. "You're under arrest!"

Wong, who'd regained his footing, shouted that he was charging Page and Kesey with resisting arrest.

"What else was I going to do?" Kesey later asked a judge. "I was raised during World War Two. What would you have done? A big Jap jumped on me. I didn't know what was happening. I tossed him off."

The judge didn't buy it. Neither did he buy Kesey's claim, as Ken looked at the good, well-dressed citizens of San Francisco sitting in the courtroom, that they had failed to impanel a jury of his peers.

After Kesey and Page had been subdued and handcuffed, we were led at gunpoint into the living room. There were 14 of us—Kesey, Neal Cassady, Des Prado, Ken Babbs, Gretchen Fetchin the Slime Queen, Hermit, Mountain Girl, Jerry Anderson—whose bride-to-be, Signe Tolle, sang with a band called The Matrix (soon to change its name to Jefferson Airplane)—Hagen, a woman named Rosalie I was spending time with, myself and three others. We were handcuffed and charged with violating California's Health and Safety Code restrictions against the possession of illegal drugs, specifically *cannabis sativa*.

We weren't Boy Scouts, that's for sure. But since we had known—or suspected, or, at least, feared—that the authorities were set to raid our little scene in La Honda, our motto in the previous few days had been "Be Prepared!" So when the squad of federal, state and county narcs and deputies came across Kesey's bridge armed with search warrants and automatic pistols on the night of April 23, 1965, we were ready. At least, naive and simple pot- and acid-heads that we were, we thought we were ready.

Faye, Kesey's wife, had gone over the place with the housekeeping equivalent of a fine-tooth comb before leaving with their three kids and the dogs: Schnapps, a mean little dachshund bitch Faye asked me to take to the pound a year later when we were living in Santa Cruz—Kesey has never forgiven me for taking Schnapps on her final journey—and Lion Dog, the wire-haired Airedale that had never been the same, really, since the time she ate a handful of LSD someone had carelessly left lying around.

(Kesey, when you read this, I was only following Faye's orders. But yes, you're right, I probably would have done it on my own if I'd have thought about it; Schnapps was a nasty little bastard!)

Faye had vacuumed stray marijuana flakes from the rugs. She had rounded up all the alligator clips and hemostats and Squirkenwerks devices that might be considered roach clips. She had even picked errant pot seeds from between the boards of the floor in the house. We swallowed or smoked or otherwise ingested or got rid of all the DMT, Obitrol, DET, Dexamil, Dolophine, hashish and other stimulants, depressants and psychotropics, legal or otherwise, that we found stashed around the place.

As far as I knew, the only grass in the place was in the jar—and that had come from my cabin when I had been sent out on a "tether" a couple of days earlier.

Let me explain. We were under what we called "spaceship conditions." Just as Kesey insisted you were either on the bus or off the bus, for this spaceship endeavor you were either on the spaceship or off it. The front gate on our side of the raggedy bridge across La Honda Creek was locked; no one could go in or out. That gate, welded out of old tools, car parts, bucksaws and odd pieces of metal by sculptor Ron Boise (of the infamous Kama Sutra statues that blue-nosed San Francisco cops had confiscated the prior year from the Vorpal Galleries), was the "airlock" between our spaceship and the rest of the universe—at least until the narcs invaded. We were, in our drug-sparked protoscientific way, trying to discover what life would be like isolated on a spaceship, cut off from the rest of humankind, fueled only by a little food and a little dope, knowing that alien life-forces were out there ready to pick us off.

We had shut off the phones, told friends to stay away and put up signs shooing visitors away from the premises.

Of course this smacked of cult behavior, although none of us, Kesey included, ever considered the possibility that we were engaging in such activities. We were experimenting. We were, in the words of our pal Hunter Thompson, riding this weird torpedo out to the end to see where it exploded. We were, in Kesey's own words, exploring inner space without the slightest damned notion of whether we'd get back to home base without going crazy.

Often, in the years since La Honda, I've thanked Cosmo, as I call God, that Kesey was more or less a benign Prankster leader. Had the chief, as Cassady called him, asked or ordered us to do something evil, would we have done it? I doubt it, but Jeez, you never know, do you?

We knew that April day in 1965 that we might get busted: We'd seen sheriff's deputies watching us, including one up on the hill across La Honda Road. We could watch him keeping tabs on us through his binoculars. Mountain Girl kept turning on the microphone for the exotic sound system we'd spread across our hillside and inviting the deputy down for coffee. The lawman later testified during our preliminary hearing that as a graduate of an anti-drug course at some police academy he was able to swear that we were observed walking about in a "floating" manner "indicative of people high on marijuana." He also testified that he had seen us using "heroin, maroin and peynotty." The prosecutor blanched.

Also, during the day of the raid some neighbors had stopped across the creek to shout at us that there were squadrons of deputy sheriffs gathering not far up the road. The neighbors, who tolerated us even if they didn't invite us in to spike their water supplies, were genuinely concerned for our welfare. But we were still those simple-minded pot-heads who couldn't quite believe that cops would really break into the home of a famous writer and his pals just because we were weird, looked funny and used marijuana. (Remember, LSD—and we had enough Owsley acid in the refrigerator to disable a major city—was still legal in April 1965.)

Not all that many people wanted to be aboard our spaceship if we were going to be busted, or if there was a chance we were in for a brush with the law. Those 14 of us "acid-nauts" who'd stayed had spent three or four days, most of it awake, on the last of the house "white cross" Benzedrine stash, watching the bus movie, *Intrepid Traveler and His Merry Band of Pranksters Look For a Cool Place*, and smoking the pot parceled out by Babbs from the mayo jar.

It might have gotten weird in there, 14 of us locked up together, not sleeping, barely eating, taking lotsa bennies, smoking lotsa grass, destroying other pharmaceutical evidence at a rapid clip. I don't know: it was always pretty weird at Kesey's, so how would we be able to tell?

When we ran out of grass, I was dispatched up the road to the tiny shack I had rented on a nearby muddy mountain road aptly named Redwood Terrace. I was on a "tether," i.e., I talked into a portable tape recorder (remember, technology was fairly primitive in 1965) during my 10-minute round-trip from Kesey's, up to the cabin and back. It was our version of walking in space, I guess.

The marijuana I brought from my place was the stuff in the mayo jar, and it went into the septic tank when Kesey flushed just as Willie Wong rudely hopped onto his back. So I was sort of surprised, after we'd been officially arrested and were milling around the living room in handcuffs, waiting to be transported down to the county jail in Redwood City, when I heard Babbs ask Gretchen, "Would you care to eat some joints, Miss Fetchin?" She nodded and he passed her a couple from a personal stash in his pocket that he had, as was his wont, hidden from the rest of us. Babbs and Gretch proceeded to eat the remaining evidence.

The narcs did confiscate the acid, though, along with a jar of roaches they said they found. But I can assure you that they didn't really find any roaches; we ate our roaches or, occasionally, when several joints were going at once, jammed a bunch into the end of what Kesey had dubbed a "nose-cone," a cardboard tube from a roll of toilet paper, and smoked the whole shebang.

Under the watchful eyes of the deputies and narcotics agents who had set up shop at the huge, round, redwood-slab dining-room table into which we'd all carved our initials and anything else that had come to mind, I tried to act cool. I wasn't cool, of course, and sort of squeaked when they asked me my name and occupation.

Like most of my fellow prisoners, I described myself as an employee of Intrepid Trips, Inc., not mentioning that just a couple of weeks earlier, after many months of life in La Honda with Kesey and the Pranksters, I had quit my job as a reporter for the *San Mateo Times*. I knew that the managing editor down there, a guy who'd disliked me, my politics, my lifestyle and my friends, would be tickled pink when he learned that I'd been busted. Subsequently, quoted in newspaper accounts of the raid in my role as the "public relations director" for Kesey's Intrepid Trips, Inc., including a story that reported that "Kesey seemed queasy" when booked into the county jail, I made it sound like Intrepid Trips was one of your run-of-the-mill big-time corporations.

I was cuffed to Cassady and put into the back seat of a sheriff's squad car along with Kesey, who was surprisingly quiet. In fact, we all seemed pretty reflective as we were rushed down to the county seat; we were facing time behind bars, and that, we were all concluding, was hard to laugh at.

At the jail, where photographers from the San Francisco newspapers waited to snap our pictures, we were all booked on marijuana-possession charges. Kesey was also charged with resisting arrest, operating a disorderly house—an archaic way of saying he owned the place where the drugs were found—and for possession of narcotics paraphernalia, a hypodermic syringe full of machine oil we used to lubricate hard-to-reach gears in our armory of movie cameras, tape recorders and film projectors.

We were locked into a couple of cells. I was in the drunk tank, along with about five other Pranksters, a few winos and a big black guy who commandeered half of the space to himself after revealing that he'd just slit his wife's throat with a butcher knife. The Hermit, who was completely cuckoo on speed by this time, took over another quarter of the cell by acting crazy, climbing on the bars, making hideous screeching noises and generally scaring everyone except the wife-killer and his fellow not-so-Merry Pranksters.

We were bailed out by Brian Rohan and Paul Robertson, Zonker's brother-in-law, around 6 in the morning. The highlight of our release was Hermit's mother's confrontation with Kesey.

A nurse at the same veteran's hospital where Kesey had worked when he got the idea for *One Flew Over the Cuckoo's Nest*, Hermit's mom threw a copy of that novel in its author's face.

"Go back to your cuckoo pad," she screamed at him. "You should have stayed in the nest instead of flying over it, you big cuckoo!"

Kesey deftly snatched the book out of the air, signed it, and handed it to one of our jailers, who gratefully accepted the autographed novel by the famous local writer.

By the time we were on our way back home to La Honda we were in pretty good spirits again. For one thing, we were out of jail. For another, our arrest was front-page news in the *Chronicle*, the *Examiner* and the *Mercury News*, where I now work as a reporter and columnist, and we were basking in the limelight. Several dailies ran my photo, handcuffed to Cassady, being escorted with Kesey into the jail in the company of a pair of nattily dressed sheriff's deputies.

We were already, though, considering the downside of the situation. We could end up in jail or prison. Neal Cassady and Jerry Anderson, who had prior convictions on drug charges—Neal for marijuana, Jerry for harder stuff—faced life sentences for being third-time losers, an early version of the now popular Three Strikes and You're Out deal. That, essentially, is why Kesey eventually pleaded guilty to a possession charge, to keep Neal, especially, out of prison. That wasn't until after Ken's second pot bust a few months later, though, and until after we'd all split to Mexico— Kesey, a fugitive from American justice—and until we'd returned and he'd been nabbed by the FBI.

After spending five months at the San Mateo County jail farm not far up the road from his home, Kesey—who'd agreed, ironically, as part of his guilty plea, to stay away from La Honda—told me he'd never cop a plea again, ever, to anything, no matter what the consequences to anybody.

Actually, both Kesey and Page Browning pleaded guilty. Charges were dropped against the rest of us. But the narcs were not going to brook any arrest-resisting, even by a hapless Prankster whose only resistance consisted of falling in the tub when Willie Wong flew into him.

We started to think about our lawyers' fees. Rohan and Robertson said they'd work for free, both knowing their reputations would soar among dopers and long-haired acid-heads if they defended the country's most prominent apostle of psychedelic drugs. But we still would need some money, and none of us, Kesey included, was bringing in any income at the moment.

One day a $7,000 royalties check for the Italian translation of *Cuckoo's Nest* arrived in the mail. "I didn't even know there was an Italian translation," Kesey admitted as he handed the check to Faye, who handled the money. That was shortly after the night that Kesey had drunk the last of the milk in the sparsely larded refrigerator. Faye, the outraged mother of three little kids now deprived of milk until more cash came our way, picked up a skillet and beaned her famous husband with it as we sat at the dinner table. (When he recovered, Kesey suggested that maybe it would be politic if we were more helpful to Faye, more polite and less demanding.)

Kesey suggested that one way to make money was to sell articles, stories, novels or anything else with his name on it. He suggested that I call his agent, Sterling Lord, and see if he could make any deals.

"You can write it and put my name on it," Kesey told me. "Write anything you want. We can probably make more money if they think I wrote it."

I tried, but Sterling Lord wasn't enthusiastic about making any quick deals for Kesey, and, frankly, the publishing business in those days was pretty stuffy. If Kesey was using drugs, he must be a burnt-out head case, they figured.

Paul Krassner later told me he saw Kesey's suggestion that I

write and use his nom de plume as "very Zen. He had no ego,"
Paul reflected. "Kesey saw that the Pranksters could use his name
as a tool" to raise money. Frankly, aside from my inability to agree
that Kesey has no ego, I think it was merely a case of Kesey the
Writer having decided he wasn't going to write anymore. I remember the day our lawyer friend, Jim Wolpman, took him to meet a
banker. Kesey wanted to borrow some money. As usual, he wore a
bright shirt cut from an American flag and his light-colored jeans
with Pentel-pen doodlings all over them.

"I love your novels, Mr. Kesey," the banker told him. "What are
you writing these days?"

"I'm writing on my pants," the famous author replied.

Which, of course, reminds me of a story. One evening, taking a
nap on the living-room floor while the endless Bus Movie was
showing—we had 40 hours of film, 40 miles of film, that Kesey and
Mountain Girl were trying to fashion into a coherent, feature-
length picture (at least that's what they said they were doing in
the backhouse next to Hagen's infamous "screw shack")—I awoke
with my head under a little end-table. I gazed up and saw that
someone, probably someone who'd eaten a few Benzedrine tabs,
had completely covered the underside of the piece of furniture
with doodles and drawings and designs with Pentel pens in a variety of bright colors. The artist had not signed his or her work,
which was not visible unless you were lying beneath it, but had
entitled it the *Sistine Table*.

By the way, I realize that it doesn't sound all that outrageous
these days to know that Kesey wore an American flag shirt down
to the bank. But you gotta remember, in those days the flag was
still...well, I guess you could say it was still sacred. When Kesey and
the Pranksters started to wear flag shirts, or when Kesey in his bus-
movie role as Swash Buckler (Ken Babbs was the Intrepid Traveler
of the title) tied Old Glory around his head like a pirate's bandan-
na, he was truly doing something extraordinary. No one had yet
designed flag-patterned rugby shirts, let alone burned American
flags to protest anything. I mean, when folks saw Kesey with the
Stars and Stripes draped around his neck like a scarf, they didn't
know whether to salute or call the cops.

Kesey had a knack for coming up with things that someone else
would quickly popularize and cash in on. It never occurred to him,
nor to any of us, for instance, to make money by selling flag shirts.
We never even suspected that anyone else would ever want to slap
a Day-Glo paint job on their old bus! I remember during the Great
Duck Storm as we cruised, high as kites, along some Mendocino
County highway one night, duck feathers from a torn comforter
blowing so thickly into the dark that the car behind us had to turn

its windshield wipers on, that I turned to Zonker and Hassler, who were sitting with me atop the bus, and laughingly asked, "Hey, what would we do if we suddenly saw another painted bus pass us going in the other direction?" It was such an absurd thought that we just giggled.

Modestly, I'll claim credit here for inventing the peace sign. We didn't pass any psychedelic buses in those days, but every once in a while we'd pass another vehicle with long-haired passengers with crazy looks in their eyes. I started flashing them the V sign, thinking of it as the old Winston Churchill "victory" symbol. It caught on. Pretty soon it was the peace sign. This is the truth; ask Zonker.

There soon followed—we're back, here, to the La Honda raid and notorious drug bust—a half-dozen or more court appearances as our arraignment and preliminary hearings got underway in the old courthouse down at the San Mateo County seat in Redwood City. Sometimes we'd spend the whole day in court, with lunch breaks at noon and marijuana breaks mid-morning and mid-afternoon.

Oh, they weren't *called* pot breaks. They were officially called 10-minute recesses. And we didn't carry grass into court with us, or even leave it in our car. We might have been goofy, but we weren't stupid. Instead of holding the weed, we all chewed gum when we made our first appearance before the judge, then stuck it under the courtroom benches. While the Juicy-Fruit wads were still gooey, we affixed joints to the undersides of our seats and were always able to reach down to get something to smoke whenever we went to lunch or on a recess. We figured they'd never search us when we *left* the courtroom.

Excerpted from a memoir-in-progress, *When I Was a Dynamiter*.

Halloween 1970
Lenny Lipton

Behind me lay the Sacramento Valley, the A&W Root Beer drive-in in Redding, a hash joint in Weed and the ever-looming Mount Shasta, the Siskyous, Ashland and the long glide downward into Oregon. Before me, across the road, that Halloween moonlit night, I heard the sounds of a rock band coming from the big old house with the Jeffersonian columns. The house sat on a knob of land formed by a bend in the Mohawk River, just a few miles outside of the town of Marcola. They said it had been used in the Jimmy Stewart movie *Shenandoah*, and true or not, the story lent an air of glamour to the downtrodden manor.

I parked next to the pasture and apple trees where Chief and Apache daily grazed, and after fourteen hours on the road emerged from my fire-truck red Volvo 544. The music grew louder as I walked across the cold hard lawn, opened the door under the columned porch, and feasted my eyes on a mob of laughing, singing, dancing, howling, hooting and jumping fiends—what we used to call long-haired freaks—people with names like Sunshine, Nixy Knox, Belle Donna, Tangerine, Sky, One-Eyed Joe, Pink Cloud, Oxygen and Gentle Waters. They wouldn't be put off if you called them freaks. They'd like it, because freaks are what they were— hippie freaks.

Zigzagging through the throng, I came upon Ken Kesey, Master of the Mystic Arts, who had learned the secret of clouding men's minds from Dr. Strange et al, sitting at a round table doing five-and-dime magic tricks. He was fooling with decks of cards, little paddles, shining metal cups and colored balls, amusing a dozen friends. Piled next to the tricks were what I assumed to be uppers and downers sprawled in a colorful heap. At first glance you couldn't tell the pills from the magic apparatus, and as you will learn, it is this and the Master's sleight of hand that kept him out of the joint.

I had had only moments to drink in the scene when a hippie jumped into the room, raving: "The pigs! The pigs are coming! We're surrounded by the pigs!" My first thought—an attempt at denial, I admit—was that this was a brother's paranoid fit, but alas, within moments we got another such report from near-naked people who had been steaming in the nearby sweat lodge perched upon the banks of the Mohawk. Bummer! The police, we were told, had surrounded us and, sure enough, when I looked out a windowpane frosted with patterns of crystalline lace, I saw three police cars parked on the lawn like panthers ready to pounce. But the music, dancing and magic tricks continued—the threat taken in stride; for these partying fools were psychedelic commandos—veterans of acid tests, bad acid, newspapers and television, Jerry Rubin speeches, Timothy Leary declaring victory again and again, police riots, tear-gassings, Jerry Lewis telethons and their parents' scorn.

In clumped a couple of properly costumed and armed cops; you couldn't tell them from the real thing. One of them sauntered up to Kesey's magic roundtable.

"What are you doing here, Officer Doogle?" said Ken. Maybe Doogle was what Ken said, and maybe it wasn't. If it wasn't, that's the only thing I've made up.

"We believe there are minors present in a place where alcohol is being consumed," said Doogle, "and we want to look around."

"Where is your warrant?" said Ken, who without so much as a moment of hesitation continued on with his magic act. He told Doogle that this was police harassment, for this very Doogle was the same officer who had arrested Kesey, a few months before, for the crime of walking a dog without a license through the streets of Eugene. At that instant, Kesey proved that he was indeed a Master of the Mystic Arts; his was the greatest magic act I've witnessed, dwarfing the disappearance of a stage full of elephants, for right before Doogle's eyes, Ken hid the dope. The argument between the two of them had so diverted Doogle that Ken's manipulation of the pills looked like part of his magic act. He vanished the stash.

Other policemen entered the Marcola House and began to slowly scan each room—looking for crime. I went upstairs and found a scene of panic and chaos, for it was in these quarters that the serious offenders had been medicating themselves. Word of the raid had created a panic, and I saw one man leap out a second-story window into the night. Others, like my friend Terry, were frantically attempting to dispose of their dope. He had impulsively dumped the contents of his baggie into a toilet bowl in order to flush it into the void. Some of those who survived the glorious countercultural revolution learned a lesson: You can't flush grass down a john.

As the police came up the stairs, Terry disappeared, leaving me gaping into a toilet bowl. I had a flash born of desperation, and I bent over the toilet making the raucous sounds of vomiting. How much better it would have been had I something to throw up, I thought, as I stared at the leaves and seeds floating inches from my face. No matter how I tickled my throat with my fingers, I could not barf and by this means conceal the contents floating on the waters below. I made all manner of retching sounds, but it was noise without substance. I sank to my knees to perfect my performance.

"Too much of a good thing," said a compassionate cop as he

watched me through the open bathroom door. He wasn't getting paid enough to look into that toilet bowl.

After their search, the police decided that this was a proper Halloween party; they saw no crimes in progress. Don't ask me to explain it—nothing is as nutty as the truth. They had had their little Halloween prank; they had come without saying hello, and they left without saying good-bye.

The magic had reached a peak when they were present. It was a more exciting party when they were there, but we didn't miss them after they'd gone.

Thinking about that Halloween night, after almost 30 years have passed, makes me wonder about what's happened to the playfulness, the foolishness—the magic in the world. Today the long-haired freaks have short hair and the crew-cut police have let theirs grow. The hippies have gone straight; they've become lawyers, stockbrokers and college professors. And the police, who, after all, are only following orders, are still doing their thing—steadfast guardians, with fidelity transcending comprehension.

Mouse Power
Paul Krassner

I moved from New York to San Francisco in 1971, having accepted an invitation by Stewart Brand to co-edit with Ken Kesey *The Last Supplement to the Whole Earth Catalog*. Hassler—that was Stewart's Merry Prankster name—served as our managing editor, chauffeur, photographer and general buffer zone. A ritual developed. Each morning, Kesey and Hassler would come by the Psychodrama commune where I was staying. We would have crunchy granola and ginseng tea for breakfast. Then, sharing a joint in an open-topped convertible, we would drive up winding roads sandwiched by forest, ending up at a large garage which was filled with production equipment.

Kesey and I would discuss ideas, pacing back and forth like a pair of caged foxes. Gourmet meals were cooked on a pot-bellied stove. Sometimes a local rock band came by and rehearsed with real amplification, drowning out the noise of our typewriters.

Kesey had been reading a book of African Yoruba stories. The moral of one parable was, "He who shits in the road will meet flies on his return." With that as a theme, we assigned R. Crumb to draw his version of the Last Supper for our cover of *The Last Supplement*.

One day, two black women from Jehovah's Witnesses stopped by the garage, and within 10 minutes Kesey convinced them that in Revelations where there's talk of locusts, it was really a reference to helicopters.

Kesey threw the *I Ching* every day as a religious ritual. When his daughter, Shannon, was invited out on her first car date, he insisted that she throw the *Ching* in order to decide whether or not to accept.

Once he forgot to bring his family *I Ching* to the garage, and he seemed edgy, like a woman who had neglected to take her birth-control pill, so I suggested that he pick three numbers, then I turned to that page in the unabridged dictionary, circled my index finger in the air, and it came down pointing at the word *bounce*. So that was our reading, and we bounced back to work.

After a couple of months, we finished *The Supplement* and had a party. Somebody brought a tank of nitrous oxide to help celebrate. Kesey suggested that in cave-dwelling times all the air they breathed was like this.

"There are stick figures hovering above," he said, "and they're laughing at us." "And," I added, "the trick is to beat them to the punch."

Kesey and I hung around La Honda for a while. We were smoking hashish in a tunnel inside a cliff which had been burrowed during World War II so that military spotters with binoculars could look toward the ocean's horizon for oncoming ships. All we spotted was a meek little mouse right there in the tunnel. We blew smoke at the mouse until it could no longer tolerate our behavior. The mouse stood on its hind legs and roared at us:

"Squeeeeeeek!!!"

This display of mouse assertiveness startled us and we almost fell off the cliff. The headline would've read, "Dope-Crazed Pranksters in Suicide Pact."

Goofy Macho
Ken Kesey

A couple years back, a woman from East Germany came by the farm. She was an absolutely beautiful woman, an Olympic pentathelete, about 6'2". She was traveling across the country and was actually studying the '60s. She'd been wined and dined the entire way. This was during the Gulf War—Desert Storm—and she'd attended all of these conventions and honorary dinners that were being given for East Germans and ex-Communists.

Because of the war, these functions had been heavily laden with military traffic—a lot of army people. Also a lot of bad roast beef. She confided to us that there seemed to be a lot of machismo evident at these affairs—that it reminded her of what she'd read about Germany in the 1930s.

Anyway, Ken Babbs and I were driving her around, showing her places around Oregon. I got out a joint, passed it and immediately she said, "Oh, no! Oh, no! I don't do the dope! I don't do the dope!"

I said, "My God! You're over here studying the '60s and you haven't smoked dope? That's like being a downhill skier and hating snow. This is one of the things the '60s ran on."

She hesitated and said, "Oh, okay."

She was competitive and started taking some good hits of this stuff. Gradually, you began to see this stern, grim, Germanic face of hers change. Everything dropped. You saw fear come into her eyes and her mouth open and go wide.

After sitting awhile, her face began to return to shape. You could see her mouth pulling up into a smile. Her eyes were now squinty and merry. She looked over at Babbs and me and said, "All over America I have been. I have seen every kind of macho. But I did not know there was a goofy macho!"

Chapter 3

Celebrity by Association

I Was Allen Ginsberg's Accountant

I started smoking in my late 20s. My wife Linda and I enjoyed an occasional puff. In 1969 we went to Allen Ginsberg's farm in Cherry Valley, and I had to bring the stuff. I actually became Ginsberg's supplier for a while. Me. Mild-mannered accountant and professor at St. John's University. When Linda died in 1971 I began smoking with a vengeance.

On my 40th birthday, my then-girlfriend threw a party for a bunch of my friends. George, who never smoked before, had a gay old time. He left for his home in Putnam County at about 11 p.m. (an hour's ride from our home in Brooklyn). He returned at 12— and again at 1 and again at 2 and again at 3. He was so stoned that he kept riding around the block unable to negotiate the ride home.

We of course laughed all night at poor George. But of course everything was funny that night. We awoke the next day to find all of the stereo equipment stolen. Burglars. I had to go back to the store that I bought the stuff at—Crazy Eddie's first store on King's Highway in Brooklyn—to get receipts for insurance.

Went to Allen's funeral. It took place in a Buddhist temple in New York (actually a temple in an office building). Mostly a turn-off. "Is that Yoko over there?" "He looks famous. Is it Dylan?" I left at noon and, when I hit the street, I was faced with a bunch of reporters and TV cameras.

The gleeful smiles resulting from getting someone to interview many hours before the service was over froze on their faces when I said I was Allen's accountant. Luckily for us all, a stretch limo pulled up and a rock-star-looking dude with incredible cowboy boots oozed out of the car with a bimbo in tow. The paparazzi turned on a dime and left me before I could enjoy my 10 minutes of fame.

Kidnapping Jerry Rubin
Leslie Meyers

Jerry Rubin asks me if I'll roll some joints for him. I tell him I don't know how but would love a lesson. After all, learning from a guy with Jerry's history would be like having Betty Crocker teach me how to bake a cake. Jerry puts a piece of rolling paper on the counter, dumps a pile of pot in the middle, pats it a bit, then turns to me and says, "Roll it like a carpet." He then licks the ends and hands it to me with a flourish.

"Now, Jerry, I realize I don't know much about this, but aren't you supposed to remove the seeds and sticks?"

He shakes his head and says, "Oh, no—I mean you can if you really want to."

The following day my friend Alison and I smoke this masterfully rolled joint and decide to kidnap Jerry at his office. We go to the toy store, buy water guns, and wait outside his office building. As he walks out we jump from either side and announce our abduction plans. Jerry immediately sees through our elaborate disguises (sunglasses) and tells us that we have to take him to the Daily Grill to pick up his to-go order.

Being kinder, gentler kidnappers, we allow for this change in plans—he was pushing it with the stop at Flair cleaners and the drugstore, though I must say I found triple-protection Aqua Fresh to be the funniest thing I've ever seen—and with our arrival at the restaurant Jerry looks at us and exclaims, "Go look in the mirror, both of you, I've never seen two more stoned people in my entire life!" Alison cannot let go of this concept. "Hey, he's seen a lot of stoned people." She asks Jerry to repeat his comment, then has to know if he really means it. With each saying of "Yes," Alison counters with another comparison—i.e., "The most stoned this decade or all decades inclusive?" I suggest that she allow for hyperbole, but Alison won't give up until with complete certainty we are deemed "most stoned ever seen."

Jerry then begs for freedom, or maybe he tells us to drive him home, but either way we feel our kidnapping is a wild success.

Chapter 4

Munchies

Marijuana Meatballs
Harry Shearer

There was a time when I enjoyed marijuana (there goes the presidency), but disdained smoking it for health and esthetic reasons. Grass and brownies never seemed like a congenial combination, but I stumbled upon the idea of marijuana meatballs, and it struck me as perfect: the flavors didn't clash, as in brownies, but worked really well together. The only time I really enjoyed Disneyland was when I would take a break every couple of rides, sit on a bench and munch on a bit of a meatball before continuing. Nobody the wiser, except, maybe, me.

So one night friends of my then-wife and I invited us to celebrate their anniversary. We went to a Chinese restaurant, had a bottle or two of champagne and enough food to fuel the re-taking of Taiwan. We then came back home, and I passed around a plate of the magic meatballs.

We talked for a while, nobody got high, and we decided that something must be wrong with the batch. Goodnights and hugs, and my wife and I went to bed around half past midnight. One a.m., and *boom!* My head took off like an Atlas missile. I had forgotten the first rule of eating marijuana: the stomach is like a bakery, you take a number and wait your turn. The dope had sat there patiently until after the Chinese food had been digested, and then, in proper order, it was served. This was the Matterhorn of highs. There was only one problem: I had to get up early in the morning to do some actual work, and I didn't want to be high anymore. I wanted to sleep. But Mister Marijuana said, "No, sir."

The battle of wills was unequal, and resulted in a serious anxiety attack. Actual shakes and tremors. Serious paranoia, the likes of which I'd never experienced before or since. "I can always go to UCLA emergency and get some thorazine," somebody kept saying, either me or my wife. If my wife was saying it, why was she using the first person? She lit a fire, bade me lie down, but I now had a case of the legs-that-wouldn't stop-twitching and the mind-that-wouldn't-stop-going-*boom!*

About 2:30 in the morning, one of us turned on the TV. As usual in those days, old movies on most channels, nothing that spoke to me. Finally, though, we remote-hopped onto a rerun of *I Believe in Miracles*, evangelist Kathryn Kuhlman's weekly healfest. A lifelong stutterer off-camera, she had a style of talking in her broadcasts that elongated almost every word, giving her time to pronounce it correctly. She had a taste for diaphanous gowns. I had made fun of her several times on my radio show. She always made me laugh.

And, miraculously, she did that night, too. Watching Kathryn

Kuhlman got a message through the haze of paranoia and anxiety, a message that the melodrama was unnecessary, a reminder that I had a sense of humor. I lay down by the fire and got un-high. She brought me down. And I blessed her for it. But I didn't send her any money. I might have been super-high, but I wasn't crazy.

The Sign
Herbert Gold

My first year in college, at Columbia, I brought a joint home to share with my best high-school buddy...home from New York to Cleveland, Ohio, the Paris of the Midwest. My friend was terrified but brave.

"What'll happen to me?"

Sophisticated, a man of the large world now, I said, "Nothing much. Oh, maybe you'll want something sweet, a piece of fruit, say."

He took a toke. His eyes went wild. He extended his arm, a sleepwalking, zombified victim of cosmopolitanism.

"A banana," he cried. "I gotta have a banana!"

Chocoholics
Charlie Davies

While living in a small college town, I was with some friends trying out some "new" smoke on a Saturday night when one of them mentioned that a local drive-in was having a "special" on Hot Fudge Brownie Delights!

This establishment offered free home delivery on orders over $5, and that sounded too good to dismiss in our current state. When we finally decided who was the most rational to place an order, one was phoned in for four "specials" at $1.50 each.

After nearly an hour (this drive-in was at least two miles away), several more tokes and an ever-increasing desire for sweets, we made a confirming call. Yes, they did have our order, but were very busy, and the delivery boy should be back to pick it up shortly. We immediately fired up a couple more joints in eager anticipation and put on some more great tunes.

About an hour later it was noted that we still hadn't seen the goodies. We somehow found the phone and called again in case they had the wrong address, or were having trouble locating it.

They re-confirmed the order, and restated that it was a really busy night but we were definitely on the list. Slight relief, but we were all starting to get a little crazy with our craving. In order to mellow out, a few more joints were started, and I think somebody changed the record.

Somewhere between three to four hours after the initial order, there were four very uptight, very stoned and very ravenous chocoholics climbing the walls. We debated driving over to get the order, walking, or even crawling. Before we could decide the proper course of action, there was a knock on the door and it was the Delivery God! Money was shoved in his hand, tip also, and before the door shut, warm fudge brownie delights were being devoured!

Super Herb
Pot Star

Where I grew up in Texas, all that was available were varying
degrees of shit-weed, just your basic run-of-the-mill Mexican commercial. Until I met K-Bone, that is.

K-Bone lived in an old house with a big extended family.
Frankly, I was scared of the guy, but he had fresh Mexi buds, as
opposed to the usual dried-up and shaky schwag. It did sometimes
get a little uncomfortable at his house, though, when tweakers
lined up to pick up crank.

One day I went to score some buds from K-Bone and I got a surprise. He had an elated look on his face and he rushed me through
the maze of corridors of screaming babies, kids at play and aging
elders melting on the couch.

"This shit's something special," he said sticking a bright green
bud under my nose.

It was special. I'd never seen a bud so bright green and skunky.

I paid $35 for a quarter and raced off to my friend JP's place to
sample the wares.

We quickly smoked a joint and immediately headed over to
Whataburger. Once inside, our bloodshot-red eyes glowed underneath the way-too-bright fluorescent lights. As we waited patiently
in line to order our food someone yelled out, "Stoners!"

It was a group of cheerleaders with their jock boyfriends. JP and
I flashed on what a bad situation this could turn into, and how we
might get our asses beat.

"Go Rebels!" cheered JP, erupting into a giant cartwheel. The
act quickly came to a close, however, when a group of drunk cowboys walked through the door.

Although JP was scared of cowboys, I knew they liked stoners
much better than jocks. As long as we didn't piss off the shitkick-
ers, we should be able to grab our burgers and be safely on our
way.

"What the hell are you people doing back there," I yelled,
banging my fist on the counter. "I've been waiting here for forty-
five minutes and I want my fuckin' food!!"

"Sir, may I see your receipt?" said the middle-aged woman operating the register. "It says 12:53 and it's 12:56 right now. You've
been here three minutes."

The Brownie

This isn't the story of the atomic brownie which was part of a batch made with butter that had been steeped for 24 hours with a pound of Mexican grass which had been imported by a guy who ended up in a jail in Mexico and who I was always impressed with because he had rebuilt his motorcycle in his living room.

Could it really have been a pound? Now that I think about it, that seems like a lot, but what do I know, I wasn't a baker in those days. Now I love to bake, especially pizza, and sometimes I can even get people to pay me to do it, but that's another story and has nothing to do with the brownie in question, especially not the atomic brownie that is not the subject of this essay.

The brownie I want to tell you about is the one that my wife made for my dad when he was undergoing treatment for cancer. This all happened in those ancient times before medical marijuana was approved by the voters. If I recall with any degree of precision, my dad was all in favor of trying medical pot even though my uncle thought it was a silly idea.

My uncle was actually a medical professional. He was some kind of special dentist who had developed an operation where he took part of a person's rib and used it to replace a diseased mandible in case that was needed. He had spent a lot of time in England, and his recommendation was for us to get some heroin for my dad. Can we look for that? Medical heroin?

Of course, if dying people could use heroin, then the AMA would contrive ways to keep them alive longer so that they could get addicted so that the DEA could arrest them and remove them from the hospital and throw them in prison where they belong. Maybe we should criminalize disease and thereby solve the health-care crisis. Anyway, he was from a country where there was so much grass (and such good stuff, too) that in the land of his birth it was used as just another cooking herb.

The atomic brownie is not its actual name. I just made that up. I'm sort of an environmentalist and I would never equate grass, which is so obviously a gift of the gods or God or Mother Nature or whatever, with anything like nuclear energy. I mean today I'm listening to the radio and I hear a story about cars being made out of recycled radioactive metal. Is this another reason to walk or what?

But the first thing that happened with the super brownie was that four of us ate one of them and then...and then...and then...all I remember is that my friends started giggling uncontrollably, canceled all their appointments and went to bed. My wife (my second wife says she wasn't with me so I'm assuming that I was with my first wife) and I couldn't drive home so we called up some friends to rescue us, which they did, and in gratitude we gave them one of the brownies.

But back to my second wife, who once told me that if I didn't get her some grass she would actually go out and get a job so she could buy some for herself. She says she uses it for artistic inspiration, but you know those addicts, they'll say anything to get their stuff. Me, I don't need it. I don't need any more anxiety and I certainly don't need to stimulate my appetite for Ding-Dongs and Yahoos. In the '60s I ate my fill. God, I loved those Hostess cupcakes and Twinkies.

I heard Paul Krassner say that the shelf life of a Twinkie was longer than the jail sentence Dan White got for killing San Francisco Mayor George Moscone and gay supervisor Harvey Milk. When I heard that, I used to wonder if the Twinkies I had eaten would eventually reconstitute themselves inside my body and eventually work their way out like a splinter that goes in real deep into one finger and comes out another one. It's never happened to me but there is always a chance.

Now my friends (the ones who gave us a ride, I can't remember where to) had a roommate who was a nurse, and after they put the brownie into their refrigerator they went to bed. The nurse got up to go to work, and since she was a nurse she ate a healthy breakfast of three cups of coffee and the brownie all by herself. I hesitate to even imagine. My wife would eat one of those brownies and probably go into her sewing room and make all the costumes for the *Star Wars* movies. Now that George Lucas has made the prequel, will he make the postquel?

So my wife had steeped the half-ounce of pot with the butter, and this was re-organic butter from cows who weren't pumped full of BST and antibiotics. But what am I saying, that maybe we should medicate our food? Wow, I am confused. We *do* medicate our food, I mean your food, unless you're like me and only eat stuff that purports to be pure. If this food is so good for you, how come I don't feel better? Well, after the butter was strained there was this residue left in the pot. Oh my God, there's pot in the pot! At that point my uncle grabbed the pot and ate the pot.

The nurse with *the* brownie in her somehow negotiated the L.A. freeway system and ended up in a room with a patient who was lying very, very still. What could she do? Nothing. She just stood there staring for 45 minutes. Maybe it was longer, maybe not. I wasn't there, thank God. Come to think of it, she wasn't all there either. After my uncle ate the pot that was in the pot he wasn't all there either. Funny how that works.

Well, to make a couple of short stories just a bit longer, my uncle took to bed for three days. He always said that it was the butter that did him in. The nurse, nudged into action by one of those hospital volunteers in a strawberry-pink dress, took the patient's pulse. There was none, and she slowly made her way to the roof of the hospital where she spent the day sunbathing.

My dad didn't really like the brownies, so my wife ate them and made a series of chairs out of wooden clothespins that she sometimes sells at my pizza parties.

Chapter 5

Laughing Fits

Identified Flying Objects
John Sinclair

One of the greatest times I've ever had on weed—with my clothes on, to paraphrase the great Miles Davis—started one Saturday afternoon in Detroit in the summer of 1965 or '66 when several of us got together to help Bo Taylor move some stuff to his sister's house in Highland Park, the little city surrounded by Detroit that was about two or three miles north of where we stayed at, in an old building called The Castle on the west side of the John C. Lodge freeway service drive between Warren and Hancock, near the Wayne State University campus.

Bo Taylor was a young man of African descent who managed our building, worked at the Wayne County Jail, shot speed and was related to the prominent Detroiter Hobart Taylor, at the time an advisor to President Lyndon B. Johnson. Assisting Bo were the urbane poet and jazz guitarist Ron English; a crazy little guy who lived in our building whose name was John Hornfield; and myself. All of us were between 21 and 26 years of age and long cast adrift from the shores of everyday America.

Driving the car, a big old Detroit special of whatever make, was the painter, Joe Gruppuso, who had also brought a bag of bright green weed to help us through the afternoon. I had seen bright green weed before and had found it sadly wanting in mental elevation properties, so I was ill-prepared for the incredible psychedelic buzz which quickly followed just a few small tokes. The whole carful of us was totally blasted, laughing and giggling as Joe poled us up the expressway toward Highland Park.

When we pulled up in front of Bo's sister's place, the guys got out and went into the spacious house while I remained in the car for a few minutes to try to pull myself together for the forthcoming series of physical tasks inside. I finally staggered out of the back seat of Joe's car, across the street, and up to the front door.

When I stepped inside I was caught in the middle of a serious war of flying objects—pillows, seat cushions, anything soft and throwable was being pitched across the room by the stoned combatants hunched behind sofas and easy chairs. I found a protected spot and joined the fray, and for the longest time the five of us rolled with laughter and prolonged our play in the living room of Bo's sister's house.

Gradually the high wore down a little and we looked around in a mild state of shock, assessing the minimal damage to the room with some relief and then breaking out in gales of laughter again. I've never been quite that blasted that way in all the years since.

Underground Paper
Frank Atwood

The three of us decided to smoke a little of that infamous $10-a-lid weed. Since we had about a quarter-pound of the commercial smoke, I decided it would be just wonderful to make a joint from a couple of ounces. Hey, what can I say? It was the days of those Cheech and Chong Bamboo album rolling papers.

The immediate problem was no Bamboo album rolling papers. Aha! I quickly determined that a newspaper would make far-out rolling paper. This wasn't just a bad idea, it was a really bad idea. We took the front page of the *Los Angeles Free Press* and put two or three ounces of pot on it.

The three of us were able to then roll this concoction into a joint...sorta. Mark wanted to fire up this bad muthafucker so he grasped it with both hands and held it to his lips. Kevin fired up a Blue Diamond match and moved the flame toward the tip of the huge homemade joint.

Hey, man, ever get one of those premonitions? You know, that feeling that something really fucked up is about to happen? Well, as the match neared the joint, I got one. A strong one. I hollered, "Wait!" But it was too late. The flame hit the joint and, now trust me on this one, it wasn't just the tip that lit up. Man, the whole fuckin' thing went up in flames. Looked like Mark's head was engulfed in fire.

Of course, the joint blew apart and Mark's lap was covered with smoldering marijuana. Soot and ashes were floating around everywhere. Poor Mark, not only did the smoldering pot burn the shit outta the head of his dick (yep, burned right through his Levis), but the ashes left black streaks all over his face.

Whew! Kevin and I simply burst into laughter. We rolled on the floor and made like hyenas. Mark somehow didn't find the situation so funny. He struggled to his feet, brushed some of the soot off—which for some reason sent Kevin and me into peals of laughter all over again—and headed for the bathroom to clean off his wounded pride.

Mark finally emerged from the bathroom, ego obviously still bruised. He simply had to restore his "presence" by showing us a gag. Well, he showed us, all right. Mark pulled out his Zippo and thumbed the flame to life. He then leaned back and spread his legs. You got it, the old light a fart on fire trick. I don't know what the fuck Mark had been eating but this was no ordinary flame. The motherfucker shot out about a foot—and in three different directions.

Mark leaped up, grabbed his nuts, and started hopping around.

Hell, the sight was just too much for us. Kevin and I rolled around on the floor makin' like hyenas again. Just about the time our roars of laughter started to die down, Mark quit hoppin' around and took his hands from his crotch. Lighting that fuckin' fart on fire blew a hole right through Mark's Levis, and the fuckin' thing was still smoldering. I thought I'd never stop laughing in my life.

Sans Screen
Ken McIntosh

The counterculture didn't really hit Toledo until late 1968. By that time the term hippie had totally lost its cachet; dopers started calling themselves heads. The first head shop in Toledo was the Lunar Moth. My friend Bonnie had gotten a big chunk of Lebanese blond hash. Neither of us had ever smoked hash before. In Vietnam we had used corncob pipes and cut-slot toilet-paper tubes with foil to smoke the evil weed, eventually learning how to roll joints. Bonnie and I decided to go to the Lunar Moth and buy a pipe worthy of her bounty. We bought an elaborate brass chamber pipe.

We went back to my place and gingerly placed a three- or four-gram chunk of the hash into the pipe. We puffed and puffed and started getting headaches, but no real smoke. The chunk was too large to ignite.

In frustration, I took the hash out of the pipe and ground it into powder. The buzz was slow in coming on, so we ended up smoking the whole bowl before we really felt anything. I got the last toke. Unfortunately for me, we knew nothing about screens in dope pipes. As I sucked, the last glowing dregs of the hash flew into the back of my mouth. Bonnie said she could see the little coals glowing as I screamed in pain.

After dousing the embers with a glass of water, she started laughing so hard that she peed her pants, which started me laughing. We laughed while she was in the bathroom, we laughed while we spent an eternity trying to find a bottle opener to use for a Pepsi, we laughed while we tried to remember how to use the telephone, and we laughed while trying to remember her address so the taxi driver could take her home.

After she left, I stumbled down to Frisch's and had a Big Boy dinner with a bowl of chili and a hot fudge sundae. When I got home, I fixed myself a Chef Boyardee Hungarian Goulash dinner and read *Head Comics* until I fell asleep.

DEVO and the Sex Pistols
Mark Mothersbaugh

It was 1978. DEVO had no record deal (although we all knew something was going to break soon). I had no money to speak of and no apartment. It was a hideously cold winter in Akron, Ohio when, out of the blue, Richard Branson, the president of Virgin Records, called and asked me to fly down to Jamaica to discuss a deal. This was it!

Bob Casale and I arrived, shook hands all around, and watched Richard and other Virgin execs roll up these huge joints—cigars, really. No one I knew rolled bombers like these and certainly no one had pot like this in Ohio.

We remained convivial, but in no time the ganja did us in. We were tripping, gone—incoherent. That's when Branson said, "The reason I brought you down here is the Sex Pistols have just broken up. Johnny Rotten is looking for a new band."

Bob and I looked at each other, stammered something, tried to hold on, but finally and unequivocally lost it, laughing harder and harder.

We tried to explain, through our spasms, that the Sex Pistols were great and everything, but we just couldn't get it out. *DEVO and the Sex Pistols*, it was all too much. All the execs were smiling uncomfortably, Johnny Rotten was in the next room waiting to become the new lead singer, and we were out of control.

Finally, we excused ourselves, went to our rooms, sat on the beds and stared for a couple of hours, sure that we'd blown it.

Later that year they signed us anyway.

Chapter 6

Higher Education

Spacey and Spacier

My first college was a tough engineering school, and I joined a fraternity. It included a crazy-quilt collection of characters, most of whom did drugs to some extent or another, and a few, including the president and vice-president of the fraternity, who did not. There were some showdowns between the freaks and the straights, which resulted in the "discreet rule." Pot could be smoked in the fraternity house, but only if done discreetly. One day, Spacey came bouncing into the house swinging a baggie full of herb. Larry the president saw him come in and, muttering something about "not discreet at all," grabbed the bag.

We followed him out to the back of the house and watched him pour out the bag and bury its contents. Meanwhile, inside the house, Spacey was on the floor laughing. He had just come back from the grocery store with a baggie full of oregano to use on the pizza he was making for dinner.

I finished up at a liberal arts school. Just about everyone smoked pot. One evening, as a group of us were sitting around toking and doing our usual *Marty* routine ("Whaddayou wanna do tonight?" "I dunno, whadda *you* wanna do?"), I had a great idea. "Let's see Fellini's *Roma*. It's been in the theaters a couple of weeks, and it looks really interesting." Everyone stared at me. "Really, let's see it. I heard it's one of the best movies of the year." I tried to convince them. Now they were looking at me like I was nuts. My girlfriend finally said, "We saw it last week! With you!"

False Alarm

I had just left a party at the chairman of the Anthropology Department's house and returned home, where I reached into my pants pocket for the film can (which is always there) to light up and relax, when I discovered to my horror that it wasn't there. Where in hell could it be? My jacket pocket? No! Under the driver's seat in the car? No! I was wearing a pair of those foul pleated pants which inevitably deposit your change anyplace where you sit, and, by golly, those pants had deposited my film can somewhere I had been seated during the day.

It might have happened at my office, where I had rolled one before I went to the chairman's house for the party. Had I left the can on my desk? I had to find out, so at 11 p.m. I got in my car and drove the half-hour to the office to see. Nope, I hadn't left it at the office.

That meant only one thing. I had dropped it at my department chair's house. Damn, I could hardly go back to his house and say, "Hey, Dr. X, I dropped a can of dope at the house, did you find it?" By the same token, if Dr. X had found the can of dope, he would probably conclude that it was me who dropped it, and confirm in his mind all of his previous prejudices about me. Nor was he likely to return it, which, given the price of dope these days, meant a considerable monetary loss. What was I to do?

Nothing for the moment. I held my breath and went in to the office the following morning, when lo, a memo crossed my desk announcing a committee meeting from 10 a.m. to noon, which would keep the department chair busy for two hours. My window of opportunity.

I called his home when I knew he was just down the hall, and talked to his gay roommate. I explained I had dropped something the evening before. Had he found it? No. Whew! Could I come by to look for it around 10 o'clock? "No problem," he said. So I drove over (knowing the chairman was otherwise occupied), was let in, did a quick survey of the chairs I had sat in the night before, and found the little can under a table on the patio.

I fessed up to my chair's roommate that it was dope and swore him to secrecy, a confidence which he appears to have honored. Narrow escape.

Disappointed

Back in the late '60s, I was a young faculty wife at the University of South Carolina. The department my husband was in had weekly seminars on Friday, with a party afterward. We were into alcohol, but nobody I knew did drugs (Valium didn't count).

One spring, there was an unusual new graduate student who had caught the interest of the faculty. He had a pickup truck with a camper on the back, and was reported to have trekked across Afghanistan in it. He also lived two floors above one of our faculty members in a fancy new apartment building near campus. They said he came down and borrowed ice from them when he had a party.

But he seemed shy around us, so we didn't know for sure if the stories were true. After great effort, I finally got him to talk to me at one of the Friday parties. Once he got started, I couldn't get away from him. I never got him to talk about his travels or where he got all his money, but he went on endlessly about his work, which didn't interest me at all.

I wanted to change the topic, so when the group next to us started talking about the legalization of marijuana, I asked if he'd ever smoked pot. He had lots of pot stories. After a while, he asked, a little too eagerly, if I was interested in trying it. I was much too fearful to ever try anything illegal, but I didn't want to say so, so I waffled around.

"Maybe someday," I said, "but not now." I was relieved when a friend finally rescued me, and I avoided the graduate student for the rest of the evening.

The next Monday morning, I heard a car drive up to the front of my house and went to the window. I was horrified to see his camper, but he just put something in my mailbox and drove off. It was a small velvet bag containing a matchbox full of pot. I was irrationally afraid of getting caught with it, but I didn't want to throw it away, so I finally hid it in the back of my kitchen junk drawer, behind the bulb baster and the package of chopsticks.

Several years later, tired and angry and ready to leave my husband, I searched the drawer in a fit of rebellion. I was going to roll that stuff and figure out how to smoke it, even if I had to do it by myself. I pulled out the bag and opened it up, only to find it empty except for two fat (and, I presume, very happy) weevils in the bottom.

Watermelon Blues

When I was an undergraduate at Penn in the mid-'70s, a friend from high school was president of the Student Council. Well, one day he and his ministers decided to use some of the council's funds to purchase a pound of pot and set up a table right in front of Ben Franklin's statue, to distribute it to the passing student body.

When I walked by with my wife, my friend invited me to have a few tokes. But they weren't just smoking joints. No, instead they had made a kind of fruit pipe out of a watermelon by cutting a small crater to hold the pot in one end, and a slit in the other through which you could inhale the filtered smoke. Pretty ingenious.

So, there I was, sucking smoke through a watermelon, when who should walk by but the old conservative professor with whom I had been reading More's *Utopia* (in Latin, by the way) once a week in his office for the last year. I didn't panic; I just set the watermelon on the table and introduced my wife to him.

We continued to read More for another year, and he never said anything about me sucking on a watermelon in the middle of the campus. My students (now, I teach English Renaissance literature) love this story.

Chapter 7

First Time

Secret Clearance

I vividly remember the first time I got stoned. It was 1969 in San Jose, California. I had been trying for nearly six months but I was so uptight and paranoid about it that my mind would not let it happen. My paranoia was not entirely unfounded. I worked in the engineering department at FMCV as a mechanical designer on the M113 project, the armored personnel carrier used by the military in Vietnam, and had a secret clearance from the Department of Defense. If I got busted for smoking marijuana I would lose my job and my secret clearance. I would have to try to start over in a new career at age 40. And I was not good at door-to-door sales.

I was at my girlfriend's house, and a mutual friend was visiting. We had smoked what they said was some very fine stuff. The two of them were sitting on the floor taking turns looking through a kaleidoscope and giggling a lot, and I was sitting on the sofa being as straight as a tournament-grade, aluminum arrow.

After a while, my girlfriend handed the kaleidoscope to me. It was one of the kind popular at the time, just mirrors, no colored glass pieces. It served to take my mind off my mind. I zeroed in on the ceiling-light fixture in the next room. The light fixture became a flying saucer flitting about and, before I knew it, I was very stoned.

I left to go home about 2 a.m., still very stoned. I drove to the end of the street, about half a block, turned left for about a hundred feet, and then right for a very short block to a T-intersection at a main street. I stopped at the stop sign, turned on the turn signal for a left turn, and waited for the only car in sight, coming from the left, to pass so I could turn left. As the car approached my street, he turned on his turn signal, indicating that he intended to turn down the street I was on.

As he turned, I saw it was a San Jose police car. I made my left turn and started up the street, keeping my eye on the rear-view mirror. Sure enough, instead of completing his right turn, he made a U-turn and started up the street behind me. The dreaded red light came on and I pulled off the street into the parking area for a small group of stores.

I was feeling really paranoid. Stoned for the first time and getting stopped by a cop. I had visions of being arrested, handcuffed, jailed and fired from my job. I got out and walked back to the police car as the cop was getting out. This was a more mellow time when that was the thing to do.

The cop explained that he had stopped me because my car was unfamiliar to him in that neighborhood. It was not an affluent neighborhood, just apartment complexes, and I am Caucasian. He said he was going to fill out a report describing me and my car, and if I were ever again stopped for the same reason, to tell the cop that I was on file, he could check it in minutes, and I'd be on my way.

He stood just in front of the driver's door with his clipboard on the hood of his car and the searchlight aimed down at the clipboard as he filled out the form. I stood by his left side looking at the clipboard as he wrote. When he came to the description of the car, I told him it was a '60 Buick LeSabre, and he glanced up at it and said, "Two-tone, light blue with cream top." My car was a solid-color light blue, not a two-tone.

I turned to look at it. Beyond the car was a sodium vapor street lamp that was reflecting off the top of the car, which didn't really register on my stoned consciousness because all I saw, parked where I had left my rather plain, old, blue Buick, was a really sharp-looking '60 Buick LeSabre Hardtop with a beautiful two-tone, light blue and cream paint job. What a rush!

I said, somewhat bewilderedly, "It's always been just light blue." He looked at me suspiciously—as if to say, "What's with this guy who doesn't know what color his car is?"—and my paranoia meter shot up another couple of decibels. Then he grabbed the spotlight and twisted it to shine on the car, and, flash!—it changed to solid blue before our eyes.

There was a pause. Then he said, also somewhat bewilderedly, "Uh, yeah. Uh, right. Uh, solid blue."

He continued looking at it for a moment or two, hand still on the spotlight. Then he twisted the light back down as he bent over to resume writing. He paused after two or three seconds and glanced up at the car again, once more a beautiful "two-tone, light blue with cream top." He shook his head and went on with the report.

When he finished, he thanked me for my cooperation and time, and we went our separate ways—he on his appointed rounds, me on my way home, thinking about repainting my car.

Jesus
John McCleary

It was my first time. Having just left the Pentecostal Church with which I was associated for much of my life, I hadn't had much opportunity to smoke marijuana. David was an acquaintance I met when I was hired to photograph his band. He rolled it in a filter cigarette after taking out the first half of the tobacco. We drove his Beetle along the freeway with the windows all rolled down to get rid of the smell. Paranoia was rampant then. For the first year I smoked, it was always in the bathroom so we could flush it if the cops broke in.

It was cold and windy, and hard to keep the marijuana "cigarette" lit, tooling down the freeway in Dave's bug. At one point, sucking on the thing, I reached the real tobacco and got a lungful. I had almost as little experience with tobacco as with marijuana. I'm still not sure if I was stoned on the weed or sick on the tobacco.

It was the 4th of July, so we went down to the beach to watch the fireworks. I was sitting in the cold sand looking up at the stars with this unfamiliar taste in my mouth and a self-conscious feeling on my mind.

It was indistinguishable at first. Then it began to sink into my consciousness—singing. It had a strangely familiar sound. Yes, I knew that tune. Religious. They were coming toward me. A group of Christians working the beach. Walking and singing among the heathens. Hoping to save one lost soul. Coming toward me. The backslider. Getting closer. I was frozen in place. Should I get up and run? No, then they would see me and recognize a sinner. What should I do?

"Jesus loves me, this I know, for the Bible tells me so. Little ones to him." Oh my God, they were coming right toward me. Was it written in the fluorescent light across my forehead? "Fallen Christian." What should I do if they come up to me? I know I'll break down in tears. I'm doomed to be a Christian all my life. There they were. Young, fresh-faced, enthusiastic Christians my own age. "Yes, Jesus loves me. Yes, Jesus loves me...." Right in front of me. I'll look away, ignore them. Are they still there? What? They've gone? They walked on. They're off to terrorize someone else. I'm safe! I don't have to go back to church. I can smoke dope again.

Generations

When I first smoked marijuana in 1963, I was a student at Berkeley, and on my next trip home to Los Angeles, I told my parents about this fabulous discovery. They reacted with horror.

"We didn't work and save all those years so you could go to college and smoke dope!"

Four or five years later, marijuana had become an emblem of the youth culture, much was written, filmed and said about it, and my mother was now curious. My younger sister, who was going to UC-San Diego, and I were home for the holidays, and our mother asked if we had some she could try.

We took on this "project" with glee, rolling a joint and showing her how to toke as we sat in the family room of the house we'd grown up in. Since it was her first time, we figured it would take quite a bit to get her buzzed, so after doing one joint, we lit another.

My sister and I were already ripped, but my mother was complaining that it had no effect; it wasn't working. So we smoked the second joint, my sister and I giggling and flopping about the couch, and my mother turned angry.

She started saying she'd prefer to do it with "my own peer group," that this was a mistake—it was probably just psychological anyway—and then, virtually in mid-sentence, as she was ranting, with her finger jabbing the air for emphasis, she stopped.

"Oh, my God," she said, pointing at the TV across the room, "everything's blurry. Girls, I'm stoned!"

Chapter 8

Memory

Forgetting
Robert Anton Wilson

The "funniest" experiences I've ever had with drugs all involved pot, and none of them seem comic when I try to write them down. Apparently words, which cannot convey "mystical" experiences, also fail to communicate hilarious drug experiences.

For instance, a friend and I took a little too much hash one night and both got lost in stoned space. We knew who we were and where we were, but we couldn't remember the last 30 seconds. We spent what seemed like an hour saying things like:

"Jesus, I can't remember what we were talking about."

"What did you just say?"

(Interlude of spasmodic laughter by both of us.)

"I think I'm having a...what? What did you say?"

"I can't remember....What are we trying to remember?"

(More spasms of laughter.)

"We're trying to...what are we trying to do?"

As the effect modified with time, we understood what was happening, and one of us described it as "a visit to the islands of micro-amnesia."

Taking Inventory
Jerry Ochs

Once, while hitchhiking across the country, I was picked up by a very nice couple in a van filled with dried marijuana. When it came time for us to go our separate ways, they gave me three baggies to remember them by. I shared my good fortune with whomever gave me a ride, causing some of them to drive beyond their original destination.

Anyway, by the time I got to where I was going, I was down to two bags. I looked up my old friends Mike and Sue. They were happy to see me and the pot because they were dry, smoke-wise, although they did have 10 hits of LSD. We smoked a little and decided to see a movie.

They lived in a "bad" neighborhood and, for some reason, once outside the house, while one of them was locking the front door, the other one, standing down on the sidewalk, shouted a question about what time we'd be back, and one of the bad neighbors must have overheard the answer because when we returned, their house had been burglarized.

After recovering from the initial shock, they began to take inventory of what was missing. The TV, the stereo, Mike's camera, Sue's watch, the piggy bank, etc., adding up to seven items. In addition, the dope was gone, both their stash of acid and my two baggies of pot.

For some reason, they called the police to report the crime, and when the policeman arrived, he asked, of course, what had been stolen. As he wrote each item down in his notebook, they described the TV, the stereo, etc. "Are you sure that's everything? Nothing else is gone?"

"Nope," Mike answered a bit too rapidly. "Definitely nothing else."

Sue, looking puzzled, said, "But, Michael, I'm sure we counted eight things."

Mike said, "No, you're wrong, Sue, just seven."

I hissed, "Nothing else, Sue. Nothing."

"I'm sure there was an eighth thing missing," she insisted, scratching her head as if to dig out the memory. The cop, pen paused in midair, looked slowly from face to face. Sue was still perplexed and refused to give up.

"If I could just remember the eighth thing," she said. "We were just standing right here adding up our losses: the TV, the stereo, the..."

"Just seven things, Sue," Mike and I shouted in unison.

As soon as the cop left, we reminded Sue what else had been stolen. She said, "See, I was right, there *was* an eighth thing."

Remembering
Nola Evangelista

I began smoking pot in college, when I was still a virgin and very shy around guys. Whenever a guy made a pass at me, I would freeze up in fear. I put this down to my repressive Catholic-school upbringing and overall fear of the unknown. But as it continued to happen, I began to wonder if there was some other reason. One night after a date when the pattern repeated itself, I decided I needed to get to the root of my problem. I had just seen the movie *Harold and Maude* and was struck by the scene where Harold smoked pot with Maude and was finally able to express the source of his strange behavior. I decided I should smoke some pot and think over my problem, hoping for a revelation. Smoking calmed me down, and as I was sitting listening to music, not thinking about anything in particular, something suddenly popped into my head. I remembered a scene from my childhood when a neighbor boy had molested me. Apparently, I had buried the incident in my subconscious, unable to process it in my child's mind. With the knowledge of this incident, I was eventually able to overcome my inhibitions. If it weren't for marijuana, I don't know if I would have ever remembered my past so that I could deal with it.

Over the years, smoking pot has helped me with the recurrent depression from which I suffer. It raises my spirits, and changes my focus. But, importantly, marijuana doesn't put me into some dopey state where I avoid my problems; instead, it almost unfailingly helps me uncover the source of my sadness, so that I can address the underlying issues at hand.

Perhaps because I come from an emotionally reticent family, I've needed some help to tune into my emotions. Perhaps marijuana helps me reach a meditative state difficult to achieve in our fast-paced society. All I know is that marijuana has healed me emotionally and spiritually, and as an advocate for marijuana law reform, I am, as Al Green sings, "blessed in the service of my savior."

Chapter 9

Radio Daze

Berkeley Boo
Lorenzo Milam

The best place to find your forgotten history is on the Internet. By typing your name at Yahoo or Deja News, you will run across the many unlikely trails you've left behind, as you wandered the ripe, green fields of injudicious youth.

"See KBOO," said the computer.

"Oh, yes—KBOO," I said. "I remember them." At least I thought I did. Thirty years ago, under protest, I traveled to Portland, Oregon to help a lady named Lloyde E. Livingstone found a broadcast station that was later to be named KBOO. And now, under the home page of that radio station, I found a reference to what we had done so long ago. It was interesting to see how the current KBOO handled their conception and gestation. It was most interesting to see that it had become a total fantasy.

"On Halloween day," they wrote, "Milam suggested several choices for call letters for the new station. The holiday spirit prevailed, and the letters KBOO were chosen. Milam helped several other communities start their own stations. Some of KBOO's sister stations bear Milam's witty trademark: KCHU, WAIF, WORT, KDNA, KTAO, KUSP...."

Now, KBOO is a very politically correct station, they tell me—my baby is politically correct!—so they will always be in the pursuit of the Absolute Truth, right? Since the story of their naming was totally false, I wrote them, suggesting that they state only the correct facts of their Genesis. This is what I wrote:

"Now that the end of October is upon us, I would suggest that you disabuse your listeners of the notion that KBOO was named for Halloween. That's about the silliest story that I have heard in my life, and I've heard a passel of them. KBOO was named for a very potent form of dope sold in the '60s, in California and the West, called 'Berkeley Boo.' If you could advise your audience of this fact, I would be most appreciative.

"And you should be appreciative of boo, too. If we weren't smoking dope at the time—or at least thinking about it—we never ever in a hundred years would have applied for that frequency in Portland back in those dark days of the late '60s. We certainly had better things to do at the time—what with FCC investigations, anti-loyalty hearings, the FBI bugging us about our radical programming, none of us getting laid....

"The 30th anniversary of the station will soon be upon you, and it behooves you to be generous with your past, even if it does involve a few disgusting scandals. Or, as Tolstoy said, 'If we don't honor the past, we cannot honor ourselves—much less our future.' Or something like that."

Flushing Toilets

In 1972 I was the chief engineer for a college radio station at a small liberal arts college in North Carolina. One Saturday night, I had the radio on in the background, as was my custom.

Suddenly, the music faded out, and a breathless voice shouted into the microphone: "It's a drug bust on campus, and the cops have a roadblock at the main entrance! Dump your stash quick, dudes!"

Since this was clearly not our regular newscast, I dressed hurriedly and started for the station. Through the dorm, I heard the scrambling of feet, shouts, ceiling panels falling, curses and the frantic flushing of toilets. As I walked into the radio station, I asked the DJ about the source of the "news report."

"I got this call a few minutes ago," he said.

"From whom?"

"I didn't recognize the voice," he reported sheepishly.

"How do you know it's true?" I asked.

"Well..."

I drove out to the main entrance to the college and found that one of the students had a flat tire, and someone had stopped to help, and both vehicles' four-way flashers lit up the night. It took the better part of two days to get the plumbing back in order, a week in hiding for the midnight DJ, and about a year to get the radio station's credibility to the point where any of us would admit working there.

Waiting for Cookies
Hank Rosenfeld

I got a job as a news writer at the alternative radio station, KSAN—
the "Jive 95," they called it. "A San Francisco tradition since 1968,"
KSAN was a wonderful place. Even the building was shaped like a
classic old orange-and-red radio. Everyone there was hip and did
drugs, and some DJs got blowjobs under the console as they did
drugs.

Every year around Thanksgiving, a verbal memo spread through
the station: "The cookies are coming." A shipment of cookies from
Oregon, with almonds in the middle, innocent-looking enough,
like they could've come from Chinatown in a little pink bakery box,
but these were soaked through with marijuana.

Someone called "The Rabbi" delivered them, and the legend
was that the dope had been cooked "in the butter," thus keeping
the entire KSAN staff flying through the holidays. The music got a
little more intense, the on-air announcers a little more cryptic. I'd
chew a corner off a cookie and completely forget about my news
duties—I couldn't remember how to rip and read anything. Then
I'd duck into a production studio and just lock the door, turn off
the overheads, ratchet up the monitors, and dance, tight and alone
in the tiny studio, to the music and the flicker of the pulsating console lights.

Once I went in there with a girlfriend who was an actual dancer
who, in her far-out grooving moves, slammed her head down into
one of the huge solid-block Ampex tape machines, requiring seven
stitches.

That was funny.

Chapter 10

Concerts

Knee High

It was 1975. I was fifteen years old and attending one of my first rock concerts: Crosby, Stills, Nash and Young at the Cleveland Stadium. My boyfriend Carlo and I were sitting in the infield, watching the show and smoking dope—the first time for me.

We were sitting close, and had our knees up, our arms wrapped around our knees. Suddenly, I realized I could not feel my legs—my knees were absolutely numb! First, I tapped them a bit to see if I could evoke any feeling. None! Then I hit them a little harder. Still nothing. Then I began digging my nails harder and harder into my poor numb knees, trying to get some feeling, any feeling at all.

As I sat there gouging my knee, Carlo yelped, "Ouch! Why are you gouging my knees like that?" Oops. Wrong knee. At least I felt better knowing I was not permanently numb in the knees.

Changed Attitude
Peter Lit

At the Inn of the Beginning in Cotati, California, a band from Mendocino—Cat Mother and the All Night Newsboys—had a gig.

During the break, they and some friends were in the back testing some home-grown herbs for psychoactive ingredients when in the circle there "magically" appeared a uniformed officer complete with radio, gun and attitude.

What struck us the most, however, was that he was at least 10 years younger (or so it seemed) than any of us. Other salient characteristics: he was about 5'2" and alone.

The slow change was wondrous as the energy turned 180 degrees from an officer apprehending lawbreakers in the act to a group of people looking at some child interrupting their party.

He got nervous, started shuffling his feet, then walked away with the parting comment, "Well, it is illegal, you know."

Risk and Reward
Darrell 42

This summer, while touring the country with an amazing band, my friends and I stopped in Indiana to see a show. The band would be playing for two nights at the Deer Creek Amphitheater.

I missed the first show, due to "lack of having a ticket," but was absolutely positive that I would get in the next night. And I did.

Anticipating a great show, I waited on the lawn with a friend. Knowing that we had some time to kill, my friend offered to pack a bowl with some beautiful blueberry buds from Eugene, Oregon. The only problem was that we had left all of our glass-pieces in the van.

We looked over to our right, and sure enough there was a brother who welcomed our invitation, provided he could supply us with something to smoke out of. He smiled and pulled out one of the headiest chillums I'd ever seen—and I've seen my fair share.

This guy was a true old-school hippie, happy to be sharing what he referred to as "my baby." He had taken the bowl back and forth across the country over the past four years at least a dozen times. He smoked it at almost every show, and had gotten compliments from smokers, and even a cop who decided not to confiscate it. We were happy to pack it.

The bowl made it around between the three of us only once, when a polite-but-annoying security guard told us to put it away. No sooner had she spit out the words when another not-so-polite-but-very-annoying security guard took the bowl out of my hands. He proceeded to take the chillum and throw it over the amphitheater's back fence, which was close to where we were sitting.

Our kind friend looked at me with despair, almost in tears. I felt *so bad*, having been the last one with my hands on his baby. He was not very interested in my apology. The thought of never seeing his prized possession again was obviously on his mind. He asked me to get it for him, and I really didn't feel like I had a choice.

Here were the problems: First, the show was *just starting*. Second, the day was beginning to turn into night. Third, the fence surrounding the back of the amphitheater was at least 12 feet high. He offered to boost me over, but I sadly explained that there was no way for me to get back once I was over. He suggested trying to get back in through the front, but we both realized that once you're out, you're out. I had to come up with a plan.

I decided to take a walk to the corner of the venue, where the back fence met a chain-link fence at a 90-degree angle. Looking at the point where they met, I realized that the slope of the venue left about a one-foot space between the ground and the fence. I thought that I might actually be able to slide through the opening and grab the piece. So I asked some stoned kid if he'd keep an eye on me and make sure no one saw me trying to squeeze through the opening. He curiously agreed.

So I got on my belly and stuck my head under. I couldn't see much, except that the venue had a huge slope on the other side (obviously, because the venue was a hill). It was getting darker, and the band was playing their second song. I decided to go for it, and managed to squeeze my body through the hole. After standing up, I realized I was on the other side.

Now all I had to do was find the damn chillum. I started to look. And look, and look. I continued to look until I spotted it. I started to walk over to it, almost ready to grab it. I was within two feet of it when I heard a voice: "Hey!" I had to think fast. I was pretty much planning on getting booted and spending the rest of the night in the parking lot.

"What the hell are you doing back here?"

"Some asshole grabbed my wallet and tossed it over the fence. I can't leave until I find it. I have to find it!"

"Okay, calm down," the guard said. "First off, how did you get here?" "Uh, I crawled under a hole."

"Well, you have to go back in. I'll look for your wallet, and meet you at the beer booth in 20 minutes. But you have to go back in now. If anyone sees you back here, you'll be kicked out."

I realized I had no choice. However, I was afraid he would look down about two feet behind him and see the chillum. So I gave him my estimated whereabouts of the wallet.

"I was sitting in between the beer booths, so it's probably over there somewhere."

"Okay, well, go back inside and meet me at the booth."

I crawled back under the fence and started to walk back to the owner of the chillum. I was getting ready to give up. It was practically dark, and I had just narrowly escaped from getting kicked out. But the sad look on this kid's face made me try it again. Not many people sneak out of a show, sneak back in, and decide to go out again.

So, crawl under again is what I did. Only, this time, I headed straight for where I knew the chillum was. I ran for it. I saw it. And I grabbed it. I ran for the hole, snuck back in before the second song ended, and handed over his baby to the kind brother. Not only did I get a big hug, but he was so happy that I found it he stuffed me a huge bowl of some greeny-green Humboldt weed.

Chapter 11

Pranks

Smoking Bananas
Paul Krassner

The office of the *East Village Other* was across the street from *The Realist* on Avenue A. I dropped by one afternoon when editors Walter Bowart, Allen Katzman and Dean Latimer were discussing a book, *Morning of the Magicians*. They were intrigued to learn that LSD released serotonin in the brain and wondered if it could be found in non-chemical substances. Deliberately mistaking *serotin*, which is found in bananas, for *serotonin*, they launched the great banana hoax. The *Berkeley Barb* picked up the story, and the mainstream wire services spread it around the country.

It quickly became public knowledge that you could get legally high from smoking dried banana skins. In San Francisco, there was a banana smoke-in, and one entrepreneur started a successful banana-powder mail-order business, charging $5 an ounce. Agents from the Bureau of Narcotics and Dangerous Drugs headed for their own laboratory, faithfully cooking, scraping and grinding 30 pounds of bananas according to the recipe in the underground press. For three weeks the Food and Drug Administration utilized apparatus which "smoked" the dried banana peels.

The *Los Angeles Press* in turn promoted yet another hallucinogen—pickled jalapeño peppers, anally inserted. All over Southern California, heads were sticking vegetables up their asses. And, at a benefit for the Diggers, I mentioned on stage that the next big drug would be FDA. Sure enough, *Time* magazine soon reported that there would be "a super-hallucinogen called FDA." Silly me, I thought I had made that up.

When *Time* decided to do a cover story on the hippies, a cable to their San Francisco bureau instructed researchers to "go at the description and delineation of the subculture as if you were studying the Samoans or the Trobriand Islanders." It was a proper approach. At the Summer Solstice celebration in Golden Gate Park, the same hippies who ridiculed Lyndon Johnson's call for a national day of prayer were now imploring the sun to come out at 5 a.m. They had given up trying to influence the Administration, but now—under the influence of banana peels among other hallucinogenics—they were still trying to influence the Universe.

Banana Tripping
David Peel

The banana-smoking movement began around 1966-67. It started in Berkeley. The inspiration was from Donovan's song, "Mellow Yellow." The first New York City Be-In had banana grass being smoked along with marijuana. My first street band was called David Peel and the Banana Trippers. I saw articles about smoking banana skins in all kinds of news magazines, and I really believed that banana grass could get me and others high like marijuana.

I even went to the United Fruit Company's New York headquarters to see if they would sponsor my band to play banana grass songs. They said sarcastically that they sure would if only I would go to Quebec, Canada and speak to the executives there.

Even the cops in Washington Square Park tried to bust me and some other fellow hippies for smoking banana grass. I wrote my very first song, "Banana Grass," in 1966 while I was working on Wall Street as a clerk for a small brokerage firm.

When I first sang the song in Washington Square, it was an instant euphoria and the beginning of Peelmania. The crowd followed me like a Peeled Piper, singing along with my new anthem. I then knew that playing music was my new way of life, and banana smoking was my new way of getting stoned.

The brokerage company fired me because I looked too much like a hippie with a suit and I was focusing less on my work at the office. Ironically, it was one of my supervisors at the job who helped bring the banana-smoking craze to my attention. I wasn't smoking marijuana or taking psychedelics in those days. Banana grass and a little alcohol was enough for me at that time.

I then went to Haight-Ashbury for a few months in the fall of 1967 and learned to become a professional radical hippie. When I came back to New York City in early 1968, I began to realize, along with my fellow hippies and straight-looking friends, that banana grass wasn't really happening; marijuana was the real thing. I learned that when I had my first joint before leaving for San Francisco.

I wrote my song, "I Like Marijuana," for Elektra Records, who signed me as a recording artist on their label, featuring it as the main theme song for my album, *Have a Marijuana*. So before I became a total banana peel, my re-bong life turned on to real sacred herb, marijuana grass, and turned me off to banana grass. But it was surely my first high fantasy, and marijuana music has been with me ever since.

Smoking Dog Poop
Jay Lynch

In the early part of 1968, when satire magazines were few and far between, I edited and published a humorous journal called the *Chicago Mirror*. As editor, I wasn't above hawking the mag on Wells Street myself. This way, I got direct feedback from the readers as well as their 25-cent pieces. There were reports in the mass media of hippies smoking banana peels, so I wrote an article for the second issue of the *Mirror* based on these reports. It was intended as satire. Here it is, reprinted word for word:

Groovy New High

Last December 15th a hippie crash pad on North Larabee Street was raided by four members of the Chicago Police Department's Narcotics Squad. Narco officers were surprised to find 25 pounds of an unidentifiable substance in the hippies' kitchen. Eleven or 12 hippies of indeterminate sex were taken in for questioning, and the entire 25 pounds of the strange sepia substance were confiscated by the puzzled fuzz for analysis.

Police chemists were astounded to discover that the mass was composed of dog excrement. The arresting officers were even more amazed to learn from the hippies they interrogated that "Doggie Poop," as they referred to the contraband, was the newest psychedelic sensation among the local turned-on Love Children.

The busted hippies were released from custody soon after their accounts of "voyages to infinity" on a few snorts of Poop were confirmed by police chemists. It will be a matter of months before Illinois passes a law against Doggie Poop. While Poop is still legal, the *Mirror* would like to inform the unenlightened about the phenomenal consciousness-expanding qualities of the drug.

How To Do Poop

The most common variety of Poop in the Old Town area is "Lincoln Park Brown." It can be found laying on the ground amongst the trees and bushes of Lincoln Park, distributed by loving doggies as a gesture of kindness. When Poop turns white it is virtually useless as a hallucinogen. Poop users, or "shitheads," warn that only fresh brown poop will do. To derive the full psychedelic benefit of Doggie Poop it must be cured. Place a three-ounce "turd" (Doggie Poop is measured in turds rather than in kilos or micrograms) on a cookie sheet in a 300-degree oven. After baking for 30 minutes, the turd should be of a brittle consistency. It can then be crumbled and rolled in cigarette papers into approximately six Poop joints—a 12-hour trip for two Poop freaks.

Novice shitheads tend to inhale fresh uncured Doggie Poop from a plastic baggie. However, this method requires a longer period before the high is attained, and hallucinations are weaker than those produced by a Poop joint. As a 17-year-old shithead told *Mirror* reporters, "The high is kind of like grooving on psilocybin, but more warm and human. To try to describe my Poop high in earthly terminology would be a wasted effort. It's indescribable. All I could say while I was up there was, 'Oh, wow!'"

Not a word of the above was true, of course. But while I was selling the *Mirror* on the street, I started to notice that the magazine's primarily hippie readership didn't understand that it was satire. Maybe I should have called it something less serious sounding than the *Chicago Mirror*. Maybe I should have called it the *Chicago Goofy Wacky* Magazine. I don't know. But the one event I remember that truly convinced me to give up on the *Mirror* and publish Bijou Funnies (one of the first underground comic books) instead, occurred while I was selling the issue of the *Mirror* with the Dog Poop article on Wells Street.

A young hippie boy enthusiastically approached me and said, "Hey, man! Thanks for that tip about the dog shit! It really works, man! And it's free!" The kid went on about how he and his friends had read the article and tried smoking dog shit. He claimed it was better than pot. He was serious. He wasn't kidding. Now that I think about it, dog shit might actually have enough nitrogen content to get a person high. Or maybe, like the banana-peel smoking craze, it was just the power of suggestion that got this kid stoned on dog poop. I took full responsibility, though. I tried to tell him it wasn't true. I tried to explain that it was humor. He wouldn't accept it. He had been in Dog Poop Nirvana. I could not convince him that it was meant to be satire.

That's the problem with satire, though. There's always going to be somebody out there who doesn't understand it. How many folks were duped into eating their children after reading Swift's *A Modest Proposal*? How many kids have adopted Beavis and Butt-head as role models? How many seas must the white duck sail before he can sleep in the sand?

There was a time when people realized that if they jumped out of a 10th floor window they would ultimately fall to their deaths. Today, though, they'll metaphorically jump out of that same 10th story window and then on the way down lobby for softer concrete.

The Great Yippie Valentine's Day Caper
Roz Payne

The following Valentine appeared anonymously in the mailboxes of about 30,000 strangers in New York City on February 14, 1969; it was printed on paper with hearts going around its sides, and each one contained a joint:

Yippie! You are one of 30,000 lucky persons being sent this freshly-rolled marijuana cigarette. We are doing this in order to clear the garbage from the air. Here are some facts:

Marijuana has been used for over 2,500 years throughout the world.

Scientific research at the University of Michigan and Boston University show marijuana to be as harmless as coffee.

Here is what an official study carried out by the British government had to say: "Marijuana is much less dangerous than amphetamines and barbiturates, and also less dangerous than alcohol."

Marijuana is not habit-forming any more than are the movies. "There are no lasting ill effects from even the acute use of marijuana," say researchers Goodman and Gilman in *Pharmacological Basis of Therapeutics.*

The often-quoted fact that pot smoking leads to heroin addiction is just not true.

"Marijuana is not as dangerous as it was once thought to be," says J. Murphy of the US Bureau of Drug Control.

It would be almost impossible to find more than a handful of researchers who would claim marijuana as harmful, yet the government and local authorities maintain the same attitudes they have held for years. Penalties for doing just what you are doing right now run up to life imprisonment in some states. Mayor Lindsay has just petitioned the governor of New York to raise the penalty from one to four years for possession. In 1968, over 60,000 people in California alone were arrested for smoking pot. Nationwide statistics to be released next month will show over 200,000 arrests last year. The law is very discriminatory with blacks, hippies and other minority group members being the only ones prosecuted.

Anyway, we thought we would give you a chance to make up your own mind. It's very simple. Just get a match and light up! Plenty of people smoke pot who do not smoke regular cigarettes, and besides you can't get cancer from it. Just inhale deeply and hold the smoke down as long as you can. You've had enough when you feel kind of nice and mellow. If you already smoke, join us when we strike again on Mother's Day by sending out 10 or more joints to persons selected from the phone book. Oh yes, one more thing, don't call the cops, dig?

The story goes that Abbie and Anita Hoffman asked Jimi Hendrix for a $2,000 check to buy the marijuana. Jimmy gave them

$1,000 cash so that there would not be a record of the transaction. Six kilos of pot were bought for $800; the rest of the money was spent on stamps and envelopes. The marijuana was divided up among various groups whose job was to clean, roll, stuff the already addressed envelopes, stamp and mail in time for arrival on Valentine's Day. Anita, under the alias Ann Fettamen, wrote about this event in her book, *Trashing*. Because the acts were illegal, she changed names, places and the date from Valentine's Day to Halloween. Our group was responsible for rolling two of the six kilos. Anita said that each kilo produced 700 joints, or was it each pound? We had Bamboo rollers, various types of rolling machines and rolling papers. Rolling joints got tiresome so you needed to change methods. We hung out forever, rolling, smoking, talking, listening to music, and rolling. In order to clean large amounts at a time, Anita and Abbie used a window screen, while we used my mother's round metal sieve. None of us ever had that much marijuana before so we lived in total ecstasy on one hand and in total paranoia of getting busted on the other.

Abbie showed up with envelopes that were addressed with a typewriter which had been destroyed, postage stamps and thousands of leaflets. We stuffed the envelopes with the letter and one marijuana joint. The leftover joints were sent to people of our choice, some friends and some taken randomly from the phone book. Some were mailed from mailboxes on 3rd Avenue in the Gramercy Park area, the same red and blue mailboxes which later were stenciled with a yellow star to turn the boxes into flags representing the National Liberation Front of North Vietnam. Anita and Abbie mailed some from uptown, and other groups mailed them throughout New York City.

Anita wrote, "There was no way of knowing how many people got high on Halloween [Valentine's Day], but we knew it was the busiest night in the history of the Narcotics Division." The story first broke in the afternoon papers and on radio. The information was scanty but there were shocked reports that thousands of city dwellers had received a marijuana cigarette with a strange letter. By the evening, it was announced at regular intervals on all the evening news programs.

A 9 o'clock evening newscaster displayed the joint, read the letter and, while on the air, he called the police, asked for the Narcotics Division, told them he had been sent marijuana, and then was told that the police were on their way to the TV station. While he was still on the air, the police arrived, took the joint and announced to the American public: "If you have received marijuana in the mail, you must report it to your local police precinct. Marijuana is a dangerous drug that can drive people insane."

Chapter 12

Other Species

The Raccoon
Mr. Howell

Growing up in the subtropics of Florida, one of the things that can be done to defray the ever-rising cost of pot is to grow your own. So we did (and do) in every available place and way you can imagine. Since much of our lovely state is made up of mangrove swamps, estuaries and barrier islands, our youthful efforts to produce clandestine crops of cannabis eventually moved to this final frontier of mosquitoes, mud and the raccoon.

Accessing the chosen site was difficult, the shallow brackish waters surrounding these islands meant that only a canoe could be landed, and all supplies had to be hauled in by hand—building materials, dirt, water, fertilizer, etc. The terrain underfoot was all knee-deep muck, black and thick. It would suck your toes right off your feet.

Mosquitoes were so thick that any bare skin would turn black with them in seconds. Massive amounts of repellent and full-length clothing were mandatory. Since full-length clothing is highly suspicious on anyone in Florida during the summer, this had to be changed into in transit,

Despite these obstacles, the crop got planted and thrived through the summer under our meticulous and tender care. We weren't taking any unnecessary chances, and prior experience had taught us that wild animals also prized our lush green stand of weed. The stand was chicken-wired sides and top so that only our hands, with their opposable thumbs, could access the secured barrier.

Or so we thought. Harvest time was fast approaching, and our anticipation swelled as harvest time drew near. The lush green of our lovingly tended plants was giving way to the purple, red and yellow hues of maturity, and so we headed out for our last sortie into mosquito hell. This time there was no need for heavy water jugs or bags of dirt. Our labors would soon be repaid in full. Ready the bongs. This time we were coming back to party down.

Raccoons are clever and resourceful bandits, which is why I guess they have little masks on their faces. What makes them particularly successful are their front paws, which have opposable thumbs, enabling them to pry open shellfish, trash-can lids and chicken-wire cages.

That is exactly what we found when we arrived at our clandestine pot farm, one very stoned raccoon, stuffed to the gills and sound asleep on his back, lying inside the chicken-wire cage and surrounded by the stumps and scattered leaves of our former dope plants. While we were quite upset, it was obvious we'd been had. The blissful look on that raccoon's face said it all: "It was good dope and I enjoyed it quite a bit, thank you."

The Duck
Frank Atwood

We stopped at a store in Big Bear for some drinks. Things were just fine at first. One friend went into the store for drinks, the other was rummaging around in the van and I was tripping on the out-asight blue sky and toking on some hash. Suddenly my friend whispered, "The Man is coming."

I kept toking on the bowl of hash and whispered back to him, "But I ain't done yet." He freaked, and went around the van to head off the cop, when this duck walked between him and the cop. I got the distinct feeling that this cop believed he had to save this duck from the longhairs. Don't think the duck felt the same way. My other friend came out of the store with our drinks, so I glanced over at him. When I turned my attention back to the cop saving the duck from the freaks, I simply fell over laughing.

Fuckin' duck was chasing the pig down the road! Yes, really. The cop would run a few steps, the duck would sort of cock its head to snap at the cop's foot, the cop would jump in the air to click his heels together like Dorothy in *The Wizard of Oz*, and then land and run a few more steps. Of course, we were cheering the duck wholeheartedly. I don't think I ever saw a funnier sight. Needless to say, the whole store was watching, so we got the fuck out of there. Still, every once in a while, as we journeyed down the mountain, we'd simultaneously burst out laughing, one of us making quacking noises, as our collective conscious envisioned the cop running down the road clicking his heels.

The Finches

In 1988 my husband and I moved to the canyon lands in Central California. Our closest neighbor was a retired fisherman who owned 10 acres of scrub brush on which sat a nice old farmhouse and a commercial greenhouse. Richard was his name and he had lived a colorful life with fascinating stories about the movie studios in Hollywood, leaving there to fish the sea in Northern California, a stint in prison (we didn't ask) and the usual macho talk about kicking people's butts.

Richard had a German temper, more of a grimace than a smile. He loved to get on the subject of the Holocaust and his eyes would bulge while he told us that the Germans would never, ever have exterminated anyone and the story was a myth.

He really believed this. He would inevitably fire himself up so bad he'd start running around his property kicking his old rotten car collection on the rear ends. He had about fifty cars, trucks and tractors that didn't run and had large dents or broken windows.   Richard also loved to smoke pot. We considered how he would act if he didn't smoke it!

Luckily he gave up alcohol years before. After we'd known him a few months he took us out back to his greenhouse. He had 500 marijuana plants neatly placed in rows. It was April and the plants were about two feet high. He was telling us that he'd been real busy knocking down all the bird nests near the ceiling of the greenhouse. The little finches got in through the gap between the walls and the ceiling. We admired his plants and then walked home discussing the risk of growing so much pot.

The next day we saw Richard jumping around his yard like an ape in heat. He was yelling and literally flipping out. We thought maybe he'd had another conversation about the Holocaust but it turned out to be much worse.

Apparently the little finches were panic-stricken when they discovered their nests destroyed, and they worked overtime pulling out all of Richard's seedlings to rebuild their homes. They even used some of the threads on his blue flannel shirt that he left hanging on a hook in the greenhouse.

Richard was livid. He was beyond livid. He was freaking. We approached him as he was about to destroy the bird nests again with a long pole. We talked him out of knocking down the new nests. The birds were done building so why not leave them alone and let them hatch their eggs? They wouldn't bother any more seedlings.

So, Richard replanted his crop and both he and the finches lived happily ever after. After the season was over, Richard gave us one of the nests made of pot and a blue flannel shirt. We still have the nest and It's quite a conversation piece.

Gerbil Power
Ken McIntosh

One late fall Michigan weekend in 1973, on our way to Saginaw, Pam and I stopped in to visit some friends of mine in Ann Arbor. I had met them at a Free John Sinclair rally and kept up the contact. They had been members of the White Panther Party, which, on its way to oblivion, had changed its name to the Rainbow People's Party.

Darby and Lee had a huge apartment in one of those rundown Victorian houses that seemed to be endemic to Midwestern college towns. Their place was as messy as most places rented by career undergraduate stoners are wont to be. Most of the furniture was second and third hand except, of course, the stereo, which was state of the art. The decor consisted of lots of books, dope paraphernalia, burned-out candles and incense residue, dead or dying plants. Dirty clothes were scattered everywhere, and posters and graffiti covered the walls.

The kitchen walls, though, were slick with grease. The refrigerator held a couple of beers, a couple of shriveled-up carrots and some other stuff covered with a blue mold patina. The sink contained every eating, drinking or cooking implement or vessel they owned, plus a colony of cockroaches thriving on the food residue and dripping faucet. The bathroom was so fetid that both Pam and I decided to hold it until we stopped for gas later. Every room was badly painted a different color. The living room was black. This black room was where the stereo and albums were and, surprise, the black lights and dayglo posters of Jimi Hendrix, the Grateful Dead and the recommended astrological sexual positions. Pillows were festooned about the room, which was dominated by a corded oval area rug and the biggest circular Naugahyde Ottoman I have ever seen. The room was lit (it's hard to think of black lights as being illumination) by candles and gerbil power.

Darby, it seems, had once been an electrical engineering major, way back in the mists of time when his academic career first began. The day after his strobe light broke, he had turned a rodent wheel into a small dynamo and hooked up a light bulb. Then he went out and bought a gerbil, whom he ensconced in a large, cracked-glass aquarium. The gerbil was quickly named Lemmeoutahere, because that's all he kept trying to do the first few days in his new domicile. We called him Lem.

Darby would put the dynamo wheel in with Lem to entertain visitors. He did so for Pam and me. The 25-watt bulb was soon flickering away. After a couple of minutes of this, Pam asked to pet the cute little feller. Darby retrieved Lem and placed him in Pam's palm, sniffing while she cooed at him. When she tried to pet his cute little head with a free finger, he bit her. Pam screamed. Lem hopped off her hand onto the floor and disappeared. We examined the damaged digit and found no blood, just a tiny red spot. Darby again assured her that Lem was really no threat; that Lem had just been sampling the salt on her skin.

Pam was relieved and a little embarrassed at her reaction to the nip. Lee told us he had the perfect balm for her injury. He had just scored some Nepalese Temple Balls.

We huddled around the Ottoman for a Himalayan high. Pam, crossing her legs, reminded me pointedly about our need to stop for gas. I must confess that I was more concerned about trying the gooey hash than Pam's bladder. Lee was twisting off a goodly portion of a ball and placing it in a hookah. Lee sat the diminished temple ball down on a serving tray beside the pipe.

We each grabbed a hose and started sucking.

After a couple of tokes, Pam's bladder signals lost intensity as she settled into a comfortable buzz. She didn't like pot, but she absolutely loved hash, for some reason a fairly common trait among distaff Midwestern heads. We three guys started talking about our shared political past while we all drank some fresh cider from Dixie cups, filling Pam in on the things that I had failed to mention during the drive up US 23 from Ohio.

While we rapped, listened to Pink Floyd and sipped the pressed apple nectar, we would occasionally catch brief glimpses of Lem as he hopped around the room. Suddenly, Lem jumped up on the Ottoman, to everyone's delight. He hopped around the periphery, sniffing at each of us in turn. It was quite charming. He then stopped by a burning candle set in some driftwood and sniffed the air, standing high on his rear legs, resting one forepaw on the wood to steady himself.

Obviously catching a whiff of something specific, he hunkered down, rotated about 45 degrees and made a beeline for the hash. He grabbed the ball in his forepaws, turning it like corn on the cob, and nibbled away for a few seconds.

Lee retrieved the hash and we all waited for Lem's reaction. Lem was masticating earnestly as he moved away from the serving tray. He hopped very slowly to the edge of the Ottoman in front of Darby and just laid down. Darby scooped Lem up, petted him tenderly and placed him gently into his litter material. Darby assured us that Lem would be fine. It seems Lem had done things like this before and, if his past behavior was any indication, he would quickly sleep it off.

Pam and I got up and went over to check Lem out. He seemed to be peacefully sleeping.

We sat back down and took a few more tokes. I talked Lee into selling me some of the hash. We were all famished at this point and there was no food in the house, so I offered to pop for dinner. We all rose to leave, putting our coats on. While Lee and I completed our transaction, Darby and Pam chatted. Pam was giving me a strained smile and crossing/uncrossing her legs.

Just as we were about to depart, the 25-watt bulb started flickering again in the black room.

We all rushed over to the aquarium. Lem appeared in fine fettle. The flicker became a steady glow. I imagined Lem fleeing with all his strength from the THC snake pursuing him. We all clucked at Lem. Lee gave Lem a little power salute and whispered, "Right on."

Pam and I left, to meet up with Darby and Lee at a restaurant after getting a motel room for the night. About a block from the boys' house, Pam made me stop by a small stand of trees. She ran into the woods to relieve herself. That supper was the last time I saw Darby.

I ran into Lee a year or so later in a commune. It was called Rainbow's End, named for a Doors song, and run by deflated former radicals. When I asked after Lem, Lee told me that Lem had been mauled to death by a stray cat that had gotten into the house the summer after Pam's and my visit. Darby had then gotten another gerbil he named Rommel, the Desert Rat. Lee assured me that Darby had reformed in regard to his treatment of rodents and that, as far as Lee knew, Darby had kept Rommel straight.

Chapter 13

Political Protest

Blessing in Disguise
Jack Herer

I was 30 years old when I first started smoking pot. That was the summer of 1969, and my life would never be the same. Everything was immeasurably enhanced—eating food, making love, listening to music—so it was completely understandable that I started dealing pot in the spring of 1970.

Four years later, "Captain" Ed Adair, my ally in the marketing of counterculture posters, tie-dyed clothes and general head gear, insisted that we take a joint oath: "We swear by our life and our love for it that we will work every day of our lives, all day, all night, to legalize pot—until we're dead, or it's legal, or we can quit when we've turned 84."

The more I learned about marijuana and the suppressed history of hemp, the angrier I became that I had never heard any of it during my entire formal and informal education.

In May 1980 I began a series of protests on the front lawn of the Los Angeles Federal Building in Westwood that would last for as many as 100 days at a time. The demonstrators would feed, clothe and provide portable bathrooms for petitioners attempting to get legalization initiatives on the local and state ballots.

On the flagpole, we would hang a huge marijuana-leaf flag underneath the American flag. The local and federal police were friendly and trusting. Often, instead of busting drunks, they would drop them off to sober up with the pot protesters.

One morning in January 1981, President-elect Ronald Reagan came to Westwood. It was five days before his inauguration, and he needed a haircut from his favorite barber. With his entourage of Secret Service agents, Reagan visited the Federal Building.

"You're doing a fine job," he told the manager, "and I want you to know that you can bring any of your problems to us. Incidentally, why are those Canadians down on the lawn?"

Reagan had mistaken the five-pointed hemp leaf for the maple leaf that is featured on the Canadian flag.

"They're not Canadians," said the building manager. "Those are the marijuana protesters, and they live down there 24 hours a day."

"Well," said Reagan, "I'll be on the job in a few days, and I'll see what I can do for you."

The above dialogue was reported by one of the secretaries in the manager's office, who happened to support the initiative. Evenings, after work, she got high with the demonstrators, and let them take showers at her home.

A week later, after only two days in office, amidst celebrating the return of the State Department hostages from Iran, Reagan reissued a World War II anti-sabotage act that had originally been passed in 1943 as a wartime measure to prohibit anyone, such as saboteurs, from being on federal property after regular business hours. So six of us were arrested for registering voters on federal property after dark.

Arrested, that is, for patriotism above and beyond the call of duty.

Unlike the five others, I refused to accept a year of unsupervised probation and pay the maximum fine of $5. (That was the original amount specified; the law was reenacted so hastily that federal authorities had neglected to adjust the fine for inflation.)

In court, Federal Judge Malcolm Lucas—a Richard Nixon appointee, later named Chief Justice of the California Supreme Court by his former law partner, then-Governor George Deukmajian—asked the supervising officer, "Now, what were these people doing there all night long?"

"Registering voters and listening to music."

"Oh? What kind of music?"

"Things like the Grateful Dead."

Whereupon the judge suddenly stood up and roared, "I threw my own son out of the house in 1975 for listening to them. As far as I'm concerned, the Grateful Dead would be better off Appreciably Deceased!"

He then sentenced me to 14 days in jail.

In my defense, I told Judge Lucas, "I can't think of a higher honor that I could ever have in my life than going to jail for registering voters after dark on federal property at the busiest intersection in the country. If I'm not willing to do that, how can I call myself an American?"

I appealed my conviction all the way to the US Supreme Court, but they wouldn't hear the case. In July 1983, I did my time in Terminal Island Federal Prison. It was the best thing that ever happened to me. I had never been given the opportunity to write so clearly, and without interruption.

In that dreary cell I composed an outline for a comprehensive book about hemp which I would call *The Emperor Wears No Clothes*, after the Hans Christian Anderson fable, in which the emperor gave his gold to swindling tailors to be made into fabric for his imperial robes, but it was stolen. I saw a metaphor there for the US government. It struck me as the perfect analogy for creating laws against hemp/marijuana. The most useful plant would become the most criminal.

And, to extend the metaphor, "Only those with pure eyes could see that the clothes were not made of gold."

I scribbled notes in my jail cell, based on treatises I had written and published about hemp titled *Everything You Should've Learned About Marijuana, But Weren't Taught in School*. That outline turned into the first edition of *Emperor*, which I published in 1985.

Without major distributors, wholesalers, advertising or reviews, the book became an underground bestseller: 400,000 copies were promptly sold in the US, mostly on college campuses during my hemp tours in the late '80s and early '90s; 250,000 copies of translated editions were sold in Germany (150,000 alone), France, England, Italy, Japan and Australia, with more translations scheduled for Spain, Poland and Greece.

My partner in hemp, Captain Ed Adair, died in 1991.

Three years later, when I was presented with an award for activism at the annual conference of the Drug Policy Foundation—a respectable drug-reform organization based in Washington, DC which had previously given awards to former presidential candidate George McGovern and economist Milton Friedman—I delivered my acceptance speech in a green 100% hemp suit, a hemp shirt and tie, hemp hat and sneakers and, underneath, the same hemp T-shirt that I wear every day (one of an identical dozen), proclaiming *HEMP: Help Eliminate Marijuana Prohibition* and, on the flip side, *Hemp for the Overall Majority for Earth's Paper, Fiber, Fuel.*

I said that I was accepting my award for Captain Ed, too. However, I neglected to thank Ronald Reagan.

For and Against
Ruth Strassberg

My memory's a little (a lot) fuzzy on the details, but I know it happened in the early '70s (possibly late '60s) since it was a combination smoke-in and Vietnam protest in New York City. Who knows, you may have been there, and I wouldn't be surprised if other people send you this story. A crowd of us assembled at the park. I can't remember if it was Washington Square or Central Park, to march up Fifth Avenue, smoking pot, to protest in front of Attorney General John Mitchell's apartment on Fifth Avenue in the '80s. I believe it was probably Washington Square because I remember a very long walk and all of us being very stoned. I believe Abbie Hoffman was our leader, but even that detail has faded with the years and billows of pot smoke. We were so stoned, in fact, that we went several blocks too far and had to backtrack to the Mitchells' apartment. And, no, John Mitchell didn't make an appearance, but Martha stuck her head out the window.

Students For a Democratic Society
John Johnson

Great, now I have to relive those times. In 1966 or so we had an SDS office on Hyperion in Silverlake. I was rooming with Mike Klonsky a couple blocks away. People would come in from around the country and crash there. Other locals would hang out a lot.

One guy decided to store four kilos of grass under the house. Mike found out about it (the house was in his name) and told the guy he was an idiot and to get the dope out of there. I did not know about this. That night Mike and me are at home, and a bottle full of liquid crashes through our window (we were on the second floor of a house). We had been getting right-wing threats and a lot of police/FBI harassment at the time. So I thought we were under attack.

Mike and me stayed up the rest of the night with a shotgun. Around 5 a.m. I hear a car slowly coming on our hill. Couldn't see it. As it gets to our house, I ready the shotgun. Something comes flying out of the car. It was the *Los Angeles Times* being delivered.

Obviously the guy Mike told off was the person that threw the Coke bottle through our window. He heard about this shotgun incident and fled the city.

Barry and the Burning Question
Michael Simmons

White House Drug Czar General Barry MCaffrey announced the Institute of Medicine's report on medical marijuana at the Community Coalition Center in South-Central Los Angeles on Wednesday, March 17, 1999. The two-year, million-bucks, IOM study has something for everybody, from red-eyed legalizers to grim-faced anti-drug warriors. The Drug Czar gave an overview of the study and opened up the floor for questions from the press.

Yours truly, though tired of debating what ought to be a non-issue but has continued to report on it because *medical marijuana is about sick people*, leapt to his feet and breathlessly reiterated the study's conclusions.

"Two and a half years ago you said there's no evidence that shows that smoked marijuana is either useful or needed. According to the science in this report, more patients found that oral THC, or Marinol, which was once heralded, is more disorienting than smoked marijuana, which we've been told by advocates for years...that smoked marijuana does supply relief for certain patients...that there are benefits for easing anxiety, i.e., *getting stoned*...for some patients, such as the terminally ill, long-term risks are not of great concern...the adverse effects of marijuana are within the range of effects tolerated for other medicines...that there's no proof of immunosuppressive...no conclusive evidence that marijuana is carcinogenic...."

As I sputtered on, the vein in the Generalissimo's temple began to protrude, and he cut me off. "I can read the report. If you will, please ask the question."

I laughed, apologized and continued. "What I'm saying is that the report seems to support everything that medical marijuana advocates have been saying for the last two and a half years and yet at the very end there's this obtuse statement: 'Until a non-smoked, rapid-onset cannabinoid drug delivery system becomes available, we acknowledge that there's no clear alternative for people suffering from chronic conditions that might be relieved by smoking marijuana such as pain or AIDS wasting....'"

"Please, if you will, get to the question," repeated the Czar, gently but firmly.

I resumed, undaunted. "Until a rapid-onset non-smokeable delivery system is developed—of course, there are vaporizers which exist—but until a system is developed that makes everyone happy, what happens to the patients who are sick, dying, are in jail or awaiting trial, who say that smokeable marijuana is the only thing between them and pain or suffering and life or death?"

I'd never seen a General dance until McCaffrey waltzed around my question: "What I need to do is stand firmly behind the report. Go read the report and take from it what the authors' conclusions are—we support them." He went on to call for more cannabinoid study and to deny that marijuana is medicine. He also generously emphasized that the smoking of marijuana for any reason is "a legitimate discussion in and of itself. I think democratic societies ought to be able to talk about whether they want to have smoked marijuana available. But it's a separate issue."

I actually agreed with him on the last point, but I was frustrated. "You didn't answer my question. What about patients who say that smoked marijuana is the only thing that works for them and saves their lives?"

He deferred to Dr. Don Vereen from his own Office of National Drug Control Policy. Dr. Vereen basically said that anecdotal testimony is not science. After answering a few more queries from reporters, McCaffrey headed to the exit.

I chased after him and once again repeated my mantra: "The patients and doctors who say that smokeable marijuana..."

He was clearly not going to respond: "I've already answered that question. NIH, FDA, American Medical Association will examine this report, and it opens the line to scientific inquiry."

In a proverbial puff he was gone, my question remained unanswered and, in spite of the enormity of the IOM report, sick people are still subject to handcuffs, prison time—and even death—for using the oldest rapid-onset cannabinoid delivery system known to humankind.

Originally published in HIGH TIMES.

Chapter 14

Sentimental Journeys

The Undoing of Matilda
Roy Tuckman

The felonious smoke drifted brazenly into the skies of downtown Los Angeles. I, the imbiber of the holy weed, drifted lightly into the confused interior of my self. The feeling of smoking freely, and privately, in the middle of a workday, in direct line of sight of tens of thousands of people, was a strange mixture of self-congratulatory respect for my courage, fear of the criminal act I was performing in "the belly of the beast," and profound gratitude for the beauty of the sunlight reflecting off the skyscrapers and the wonder of existence.

It was my lunch hour, a rigidly defined period of time in this civil service environment. Yes, I was into the whole thing, with house, tie, freeway commute and, of course, a comfortable salary and future. Financial future, that is. The other part was bleak. The so-called '60s, for me and others, was not a celebration of peace and love with hearts and flowers. Added to the mix was Vietnam and so many political assassinations. In the mix was the realization that all our major political leaders considered us the enemy. We were threatening "*their America*." But of course it was forgotten that *they* were destroying us.

Pot is a gateway herb of sorts. It is a gateway into the land where you see for yourself, in your own experience, that your society is a liar. We are already being told that "war is peace" and "black is white." And so, many sought to supplant this fallen leadership. And there were choices to make that our parents would not have dreamed of.

And now, after 2-1/2 years of nearly total abstinence (I shared one joint one time), I was testing the waters to see what I had missed, if anything, and if it were to be reintegrated into my life. After 2-1/2 years of psychiatric drugs and a radical squarization process, I was contacting the memory of the acid-inspired insights of the past to ask for a judgment on my life. Matilda helped me with the answer.

Matilda was the bane of the office. She was an attractive woman who strove to live up to the stereotype of the "hot Latina." Before you start salivating, let me add that there was no sexual component to her temperature. But she was professional in her ability to stop the office cold with her shrieks and cries, brought on by the least perceived slight, or criticism, or any of the slings and arrows that jobs are prey to. And with this emotionalism, Matilda ruled the office from her secretary's desk, rattling at will even the second-in-command of the entire department. I don't recall what it was about me that motivated Matilda to aim at me. I must have been a quiet and pleasant, if slightly depressed type.

And I was square, absolutely square. And there was certainly no racial component in this relationship. My graduate years in anthropology had specialized in the study of the astounding cultures of Mexico and Central America, and I had only the greatest respect for her ancestry. I had climbed El Castillo in Yucatan (before Raquel Welch), and passed my graduate Spanish exam at UCLA. I never insulted her, but I never bowed to her, either. I was living with a real woman, and considered Matilda's childish games to be, well, childish games. She probably found that approximately unforgivable. Fortunately, most of my job was out of the office, so relief was just a few steps away.

I looked at my watch—my schizophrenic watch, that is. I often told people that the two shimmering spider turquoise stones ornamenting the band were a second watch, telling the real time, which is always Now. But my chronometer dictated that it was time for me to go back to work. So I disposed of the rest of the joint— in those days it was by eating the rest of the marijuana but not (usually) the paper—and left the roof of my downtown office building, descended the stairs, washed my hands, combed my short hair, straightened my tie and sat down in my shared office cubicle with my papers and adding machine.

Matilda came prancing down the office aisle, carrying a load of 3x5 cards. She would soon walk past the 3-foot wide entrance to my cubicle. I sat at my desk in absolute calm, glowing from the rooftop experiment, and enthusiastically planned the rest of my day, and my life. Then she screamed: "Ohhhhh!"

Matilda had tripped or otherwise slanted her office-supply burden, and a stream of dozens of 3x5 cards slipped out of her hands and all over the floor around my desk and chair. The shrill woman whose pride would have done credit to an Aztec headdress was forced to crawl and grovel all around my office for several minutes.

The victory was too obvious for me to feel any sense of revenge, accomplishment or satisfaction. I felt compassion for her plight, although, in my memory, my compassion did not extend to actually helping her to pick up the cards. But I was a beginner, as I am now. And there were other cards being dealt, cards foretelling my future and my relationship with marijuana, and the meaning of my psychedelic years. In one second, while I was busy in relaxed and joyful contemplation, the number one office problem had been solved for me. Matilda would never again try to goad me. We both knew that the war was over and we had witnessed the final battle. I knew, although she didn't, that I credited the Spirit of the Herb, whatever that was, with this little adventure, as a sign that the herb was an ally, not an enemy, and our separation would end.

The Midwife
Dew U. Care

Oh, I suppose it was a miracle. An act of love that began with a line of poetry, climaxed in the back seat of an economy-sized car, and culminated in the birthing of a babe.

The midwife and husband stood at the ready, humbled by the complicated simplicity of the event. Unlike examples of women who'd paused in their labor, squatted in a field, commenced with a more personal type of labor, then bit the cord that binds—and with babe on back, went back to the other labor. Madelaine's had been going on for 23 hours.

Perhaps it was because it was her first child. Maybe it was her narrow pelvis. Or perchance the months of abstinence, having given up cigarettes, wine, coffee, pot, dying her hair and all her favorite clothes, made her unable to give up one more thing. But we can state for a fact that the mother-to-be was not gently glowing and sweetly gasping as in the movies, she was sweating pools and cussing in three different languages. "Fuck! Mon Deu! Mon Deu! Oh, pinche tu madre! Help! Oh, I told you that you shouldn't have cut off the end of the condom because it was too long!"

"Breathe," said her life partner gently.

"If you're so damned hot on breathing, *you* breathe!"

"Now, darling, you were great during the Lamaze classes."

"Dr. Lamaze was a man. I want drugs!"

"Now, sugarplum, you were the one who wanted a natural birthing experience."

The friend operating the video camera nodded his head in agreement.

"Why don't you all just die?" the lady was heard to ask (all present gave the lady the benefit of the doubt and assumed the question was rhetorical). The midwife counseled, cajoled, massaged in ointments, wiped the woman's brow with linen dipped in aromatic herbs. She related stories of easier births, then she told of more difficult ones. She recited Haiku and Bible verses and African birthing stories. To no avail. The uterus dilated, the contractions increased, as did everyone's frustration. Yet the babe refused to come until, it seemed, conditions known only to it were met.

The midwife consulted with the husband. An ambulance would take the woman to the hospital if the birth was not started soon. This was not the unthinkable alternative it had been just 24 hours earlier.

Midwifery is as much an art as a science, and the midwife whispered, promised, cajoled, sang, massaged some more, for she wanted to be the one to bring the babe into the world. She whispered in the woman's ear, "Let go of the gift and I will roll you a joint the likes of which you've never seen. Not just any joint, but a spleef rolled from the tips of buds grown in *campo sancto* by monks, blessed by a rabbi, and wrapped in organic rice paper by the delicate fingers of an aged Tibetan sage. It's six inches long and as fat as..." Here she cast a flirtatious look at the flushed life partner, who if possible, looked even more bedraggled than his lady love.

"Give it to me now," gasped the poor mother-to-be.

"No, my sweet. No substance shall pass your lips until you deliver what you've brought to me to be delivered."

"Don't make me get off this table," yelled the lady.

"No. Only afterward. That is the deal. I don't negotiate. If you have to go to the hospital, you'll be in a cold, sterile environment where the sacred smoke is not welcome and they serve bad coffee to boot."

And we, gentle reader, will never know if it was the babe's own sweet time, the deity's will, or the promise of some truly righteous weed, but it did come to pass...literally, and the mother was delivered of a beautiful bouncing baby girl.

The midwife made good her promise and delivered the sacred spleef.

And then the third miracle occurred (the first being the conception, the second the birth)—no one told the new mother to pass on the joint. And yet she shared the sacred six inches of her own volition.

And what of the babe, hallowed by the halo of sacred smoke? She grew into a wise, brilliant, beautiful, kind, very patient and calm woman—who likes her wine, her cigarettes, her coffee and her herb.

The Blind Mime
Dew U. Care

It was a blind boy who brought me to pot, and I never had the foresight to thank him.

It was my junior year in college and I was floundering about, looking for a major that would carry me through life. As if. But one is young and impressionable, and in my trying out of various guises, I worked with Handicapped Student Services. Part of my job entailed reading to visually-impaired students.

My favorite was a boy named Bob. Bob had a "photographic" memory, an incredible audio retention. He could hold hundreds of bits of information at once (i.e., retain a 50-question multiple-choice quiz, each with five possible selections). A psychology major, Bob also had the ability to generate amazingly original ideas. Add to that a wry sense of humor, a kind heart, and the sweet, good-natured, broad-shouldered "Gee, ma'am, are my boots under your bed?" charm the South is known for, and you have Bob.

Sitting on the grass, Bob pulled out a joint. I stared. Then I quickly got over it. Bob could always seem to tell when I was staring.

"But that's illegal," I gasped.

"No, it's okay, really. I use it for medicinal purposes. It keeps me from going blind."

"Ah...Bob..."

"Yes?"

"...um...um...you *are* blind."

"You're right." Pause. He screams. Other people turn around. Bob continues. "I can't see! I can't see! I'm blind!" People continue to stare. Bob puts his hands in front of him. No! No! Anything but this!

It's his Mime in a Box, because in a misguided moment of compassion I had encouraged him to distract himself from his Humphrey Bogart and Bob Marley and Bette Davis impressions. How was I to know he'd keep at it? Then he sat down.

"Look," he said, "I've enjoyed pot for five years. I'm getting into grad school. Science, the scientific method, is my forte. Pot has never been proven, after decades and decades of research, to have detrimental attributes. On the contrary. Most scientific and anecdotal evidence leads to the opposite conclusion. The most harmful thing for your body is stress and depression.

"Smoking pot enhances my perceptions and appreciation for the world around me. Okay, maybe I shouldn't pilot an airplane, go through a pregnancy, or perform neurosurgery under it, but you've got my word of honor that I wouldn't dream of doing any of those three things under the influence of THC. Scout's honor."

"Uh, Bob, are you a Scout?"

"While I did say 'Scout's honor,' I never by word or deed, only the assumptions you brought, said I was the Scout in question."

"But if marijuana were okay, it'd be legal now."

"Segregation was legal in this country until the '50s. Gay legal rights are still iffy. And an amendment that said women were equal was struck down. We do funny things. But I do believe that we're evolving as a species. Continually maturing. By my reckoning, we're in our adolescence. Some day future generations will look back at pot prohibition with the same proper horror with which we view bloodletting."

"But I'm afraid it will interfere with my ambition," I said.

"I've been meaning to tell you, you're a type-A personality. You bite your nails. I can hear you, you know. Shouldn't nibble on the cuticle like that."

I pulled my finger out of my mouth.

"You mean I'm a type-A because I bite my nails?"

"No, you bite your nails because you're a type-A."

Here he broke off into his Groucho Marx imitation, complete with ashing an imaginary cigar.

"And I don't mean a blood type. I mean a tenseness. Let me put it another way. Are you usually the first person on and off an elevator?"

"Yes, why?"

"Even though you know it's not going to move until the last person's on, you'll push and pull and weave and elbow and stand stubbornly in the front?"

"Yes, what's your point?"

"Do you understand the oxymorons of 'trying to relax,' 'military intelligence,' 'right-to-work-state'? Are you the same religion, voting, economic status as your family?"

Silence, as I pulled on the loose hem from my shorts-from-Sears in a charming pastel color.

"Here," he said, "try a hit. Hold it for a bit, exhale gently. Ready, set, go!"

And with that he handed me The Torpedo.

First it was the scent that intoxicated me, fresh and vital, musky and straw-like, yet with sweet overtones. Then it was the way the ember flared as I pulled the warm spring air and the smoke into my lungs. The sound of wind blowing through the leaves and grass. I closed my eyes.

I experienced the world through my other senses. I tried to experience the world as Bob did.

Through the years our lives took different roads, and the paths we'd chosen seldom crossed. Bob never did work with the differently-abled, as he'd planned then, except as a volunteer. He worked as a lawyer for various progressive causes, his family growing—last time we met he had a seeing-eye dog in the lead and his youngest taking up the rear in a royal red papoose pack.

"During my act I tell people I'm their worst fear in a packed airplane—the guy with the kid and the dog."

"You do stand-up?"

"Yeah, I added it to my mime routine. Mime in a Box!"

"How do you find the energy?"

For an answer he pulled *The Torpedo* out of his coat pocket.

I looked at him fondly. We'd known each other many moons. I took the spleef and the smoke and the shared memories and held them deep. I closed my eyes. I felt his arm around my shoulders. I sighed with satisfaction. Then I handed him the joint.

"My little pothead," I said. "I think I'll keep him."

The Funeral
Dew U. Care

As funerals go, I suppose it went well enough. No one threw themselves at the casket, the religious leader I'd rented for the occasion
mouthed the words I'd fed him with a passable sincerity, no one
barfed at the wake—at least not in the hall itself—and the check
I'd written for the whole shebang cleared. All-in-all, a success—as
such things go.

Now, where there's a will there's a way. Usually your way, my
way, Yeoway's, or the highway. Which brings us to the subject of
my story, my beloved sister. The good Lord has a sense of humor,
no one can take that away from him, but there has to be a rhyme
and reason for the madness around us, and my madness has included going through life a clone—an identical twin.

I've grown up with a pair of eyes that mirror my own staring
back at me, a gallery of similar gestures, a certain stride that marks
us—and that's it. My Republican, "free the magic of the market-
place," MBA/lawyer sister is to me like the cream in my coffee (i.e.,
the scum that rises to the surface). In her patented manner, she lost
herself in grief until I'd taken care of the funeral, only to find herself in time for the division of the estate.

I've never minded my sibling's single-minded self-interest. All
right, I have, but there's a difference between ideological differ-
ences and being dicked over in the particular. We all can't cuddle
orphans, pen sonnets, bake bread, comfort the dying. Some of us
were made for other things—mergers, acquisitions, takeovers and
litigation, for example. Some of us frolic with the dolphins and
others swim with the sharks. And that's okay—or at least it was
until she stole from me. Even then I didn't take it personally. You
can only steal what you have access to. And what she had access to
was me.

During the probate period, money, stocks, bonds, certificates of
deposit, and just about anything worthy of a serial number disappeared as quietly and efficiently as a Central American dissident.

But then the bitch absconded with our parents' wedding bands.
Feigning innocence, she prevaricated, stalled, stonewalled and
then flat-assed-out lied.

My first impulse was to...well, it's pretty much unprintable, and
may be in fact a physical impossibility to bend an appendage to an
orifice in quite the manner I'd contemplated, so I went for my second impulse. I got stoned. Then I got her stoned. Now at this ston-
ing, stamina came into play. You just can't compete with a hard-
core ounce of red-haired bud a month. I was hitting my stride as
she slid under the table. I was wetting my lips with an innocent pink

tongue while her parched lips went through contortions. And in exchange for a package of Hostess products and some pizza-flavored potato chips, she caved.

It was Jacob and Esau updated. Only, instead of the pot of thick porridge for the birthright, I got her stoned and let her walk away with her integrity—and her life.

"I took the wedding rings," she sobbed, chocolate rimming the corner of her lips, nacho crumbs in the lapels of her Armani.

"Honey, I knew you did."

We hugged. We kissed. In the morning she woke up with a fresh conscience. I had helped her to do the right thing. Sure, I had to weed her up to do it, but as Voltaire wrote, "Cultivate your garden." Happily, my garden grows a righteous weed.

Chapter 15

Disneyland

Peer Pressure
Bob Wieder

In 1972 I went with a bunch of friends from a Berkeley anarchist collective to Disneyland, where we all got stoned.

There was one slow, pseudo-ride called the People Mover that was more an elevated tour of Tomorrowland than an actual attraction. It made two leisurely passes through (and overhead) the spacious Tomorrowland gift shop.

On our first pass, we all started calling out at the shoppers: "Buy! Consume! Spend!"

A few minutes later, we made our second pass, and repeated our cheers. Only, this time, all the people shopping in the store joined in, evidently with no sense of sheepishness or irony, yelling: "Buy! Consume! Spend!"

Fickle Finger of Fate
Waldo Steve and the Waldos

In the early '70s, the young Waldos—a group of friends from Marin County, California—were planning a stoner's trip to Los Angeles and Disneyland. We were planning it for weeks. The day before the trip, two of the Waldos phoned me in the afternoon and said they could not go because they did not have the cash. No money, no trip. A big letdown. About nine that same evening, I got a surprise phone call from the two cashless Waldos. They said, "We can go now! We have lots of money. Wait at your house and we will come right over to explain." When they arrived, they got out of the car holding brown-paper shopping bags. Because my parents were having a party in the front of the house, we went around the side gate, through a back door and into my room, unnoticed. As soon as the door was closed and locked, they opened the shopping bags and started pulling out and throwing cash in the air. I joined in, reaching into the bags, grabbing fistfuls of money and throwing it into the air. It was raining money, and the floor was completely covered with green bills. The previously cashless and now rich Waldo explained that he had suffered for a long time while working for an ex-boss, who was an extremely abusive asshole. And this money was a revenge-related windfall.

The next morning we packed up my 1966 4-door Chevy Impala (with a killer Craig 8-track stereo system) to head for Southern California. The cargo consisted of four guys and a girl with long brown hair, named Laura, who needed a lift to L.A. The cargo also consisted of six lids of fresh green smoke.

Driving south on Highway 101, we were in a hurry because I was extremely determined to make it to Burbank (to be an audience member) for an afternoon taping of the *Tonight Show* with Johnny Carson.

Unfortunately I had to slow down. Around San Luis Obispo, a police car got onto the highway directly behind us. I warned my passengers to put out their joints. However, my passengers thought it was sufficient to just keep the joints down low.

A second police car entered onto the highway in front of us. Now there was one cop in front and one in back of us. Besides the police, we were the only car on the freeway. We put out the joints and watched the speedometer.

Within minutes, more cop cars entered onto the highway. Two behind us and two in front of us. Then, three squad cars behind us and three in front of us. We put the lids down our pants and continued to drive the speed limit. Then the cop car directly behind us lit up his bright flashing colorful lights.

We pulled over to the side of the road and so did all six squad cars. The officers jumped out and pulled their guns but did not approach our car. Stoned, we sat and waited for 10 minutes while the officers walked around at a distance. Would we be busted?

An officer approached the car and asked for all of our licenses. He took the IDs back to his car and we waited. We waited for a full half-hour in total suspense inside our reeking automobile. Would we be busted?

The officer came back to our car, handed me our drivers' licenses and said we could go free. I questioned him about our detainment. He said the cops thought that the girl in our car was Patty Hearst and that we were the SLA (Symbionese Liberation Army) headed south.

Very stoned, and very miffed about the delay, I then reprimanded the police officer, saying, "You goof, now we're going to miss Johnny Carson."

We got to Los Angeles in the early evening and went to a motel to try to get a room. They had no vacancies. The second, third, fourth, fifth, sixth and seventh motels we tried also had no vacancies.

With no other options, we filled up the gas tank. Gasoline was only about 40 cents a gallon and we had six lids of grass. Nonstop, we cruised the freeways of L.A., continuously smoking weed until the sun came up. Cheaper than a motel.

Later that morning, the Waldos arrived at Disneyland determined to smoke out everywhere in the park. And we did. At one point we hopped a fence, ran up a little hill and down into a phony Disney-created desert scene. Consisting of a few acres, it was made to look like Arizona or Utah. We smoked out all over the phony little Southwest.

A train whistle blew. There was a train tunnel leading to our Southwest desert mockup. Happy Disney customers were all aboard and quickly coming our way. We ran up a hill and hid behind a giant red phony rock. Crouching tightly behind the boulder, we lit up a new joint. The train stopped in the middle of the desert.

The tour guide on the train pointed directly at us as he exclaimed to the passengers, "Oh, my!" All eyes on the train looked right at us. We froze still. The tour guide then continued, "Oh, my! It's Old Faithful!"

Suddenly, about two feet from my right foot, a water geyser shot up. Two feet high, six feet high, 15 feet high. The Waldos took a good soaking. The train drove away. We were soaked, but we didn't spoil the vacation for the Disney customers.

The Disneyland Memorial Orgy
Paul Krassner

When Walt Disney died in December 1966, I remembered a couple of his statements with peculiar affection. "I love Mickey Mouse," he had once said, "more than any woman I've ever known." In 1945, Aldous Huxley went to work for him as a consultant on the filming of *Alice in Wonderland*. There was gossip that Huxley had turned him on with magic mushrooms. "If people would think more of fairies," Disney said a year later, "they would forget the atom bomb."

There were rumors that Disney's body had been frozen, although it was actually cremated. Somehow I had expected Mickey and Donald Duck and all the rest of the gang to attend the funeral, with Goofy delivering a eulogy and the Seven Dwarves serving as pallbearers. After his death, as a personal pilgrimage, I thought it would be appropriate to visit Disneyland. I went with three friends, one a lawyer whose dog jumped into the car as we were leaving his home. We ate marijuana brownies for the occasion.

Dogs were not allowed in Disneyland. In fact, male humans with long hair or beards or other stereotypical hippie accouterments were not allowed in. The Beatles, who were more popular than Christ, would not have been permitted to enter Disneyland—unless they were performing there. Indeed, Jesus himself would not have been permitted to enter Disneyland—unless *he* was performing there.

We bluffed our way into Disneyland by convincing a ticket-taker that the manager had given us permission earlier on the telephone inasmuch as the dog was needed to guide my friend with the impaired eyesight. Inside, we continued to fake it, explaining that the dog had already been cleared by the ticket-taker.

After lunch, a large man with a small walkie-talkie approached us with the choice of putting the dog in the Disneyland kennel or leaving the place altogether. My friend explained how this exception to their rule had been arranged two weeks ago, and he asked to speak to "the chief of security."

"I *am* the chief of security."

"Ah, just the man I want to see."

Incidentally, I should mention that the canine in question was *not* a seeing-eye dog (which would now be called an assisted-living dog). It wasn't even a German shepherd. There was no metal brace for the owner to hold on to, just a rotten, knotted leather leash. Moreover, the dog was a bloodshot-eyed basset hound that kept stumbling all over the ground because it had to pee and was searching for a spot where a dog had previously peed, any dog, but no dog had ever peed in Disneyland. Especially not Pluto.

Okay, then, if we had to leave, were we not entitled to a full refund? Yes, we were. So, while the others waited at the gate, I was escorted to a building called City Hall. There, a woman was requesting that her lost child be paged over the loudspeaker, but she was refused because it wasn't considered an emergency.

I didn't wish anyone to think that I wanted them only for their money, so I asked if there had been any special ceremony when Walt Disney died.

"No, we kept the park open. We felt that Mr. Disney would have wanted it that way."

"Well, wasn't there *any* official recognition of his passing?"

"We did fly the flag at half-mast for the rest of the month."

Disney stock rose one point the day after his death and continued to ascend. The company earned $100 million the next year, and even though Disney was dead, Mickey Mouse would continue to bask in his own immortality. Disney's death occurred a few years after *Time* magazine's famous "God Is Dead" cover, and it struck me that Disney had indeed served as God to Mickey, Donald Duck, Goofy—that whole stable of imaginary characters who were now mourning in a state of suspended animation. Disney had been *their* Creator and he had repressed all their baser instincts, but now that he had departed they could finally shed their cumulative inhibitions and participate together in an unspeakable Roman binge, to signify the crumbling of an empire. I assigned *Mad* magazine artist Wally Wood to create—as a centerspread for *The Realist* which later became a poster—the infamous Disneyland Memorial Orgy.

Pluto was pissing on a portrait of Mickey Mouse, while the real, bedraggled Mickey was shooting up heroin with a hypodermic needle. His nephews were jerking off as they watched Goofy fucking Minnie Mouse on a combination bed and cash register. The beams shining out from the Magic Castle were actually dollar signs. Dumbo was simultaneously flying and shitting on an infuriated Donald Duck. Huey, Dewey and Louie were ogling Daisy Duck's asshole as she watched the Seven Dwarves groping Snow White. The Prince was snatching a peek at Cinderella's snatch while trying a glass slipper on her foot. The Three Little Pigs were humping each other in a daisy chain. Jiminy Cricket leered as Tinker Bell did a striptease and Pinnochio's nose got longer.

And so, still thoroughly stoned, we left Disneyland to fend for itself.

Originally published in HIGH TIMES.

Chapter 16

Amsterdam

Space Cake

I smoked a lot of dope in college. I had my reasons. I went to an engineering school. In Cleveland. At the outset of the Reagan years. Women were outnumbered on campus by more than three to one. Almost all of my potential male friends played Dungeons & Dragons.

This was even more depressing than it sounds. So my roommate and I kept the bong lit and the Firesign Theater records playing, and we prayed for graduation or death. This was the entire extent of my drug use in school. Once I got out and around some actual women, my interest in marijuana ended.

Fast forward 10 years. By 1994, I was living in a beach house in Santa Monica with a beautiful, sweet, funny woman named Mindy. We intended to marry some day, and we filled the interim by inventing new sexual practices and naming them after states where we thought they would be illegal.

This was great for public flirting. We would stand in line at a drugstore checkout, and I would lean over and whisper the word "Mississippi," and we would both be titillated for an hour until we got home and actually committed that crime. This was true love.

At least until Christmas Eve, when Mindy told me (and I swear this is true) that she had been sleeping with another guy, didn't know why, and she was therefore going to sort things out by moving to Ecuador.

I started smoking dope again.

Fast forward six more months. In summer 1995, I was killing time by riding trains around Europe. I had stopped smoking weed again. Instead, I spent most of my free time hanging around historic churches and cathedrals. Not because I'm religious; because they're remarkably good places to pick up women, who are often so awestruck and reverent that they don't realize you have a plan.

I once spent a whole week cruising the Vatican, trying to score chicks from every member of the Warsaw Pact. None of this made me forget the thing Mindy could do with her teeth that we called "Louisiana."

One day, I was in Paris, paying my respects to Jim Morrison and wondering if it would be nice to be buried in Pere Lachaise. My travel agent, who had once been *our* travel agent, told me that Mindy was visiting Amsterdam.

The next day, so was I.

Mindy and I hooked up in a place called the Boatel, a stationary Love Boat docked near the Centraal train station. Our window was at water level, and seagulls ate bread from our hands.

Except for the fact that we had nothing to say to each other, it was romantic as hell. So, then. What to do? See the sights, we decided. Specifically, there were three places Mindy wanted to visit: a flower market where she could buy some souvenir tulips; the Anne Frank house; and the Oude Kirk, a big old church Mindy was interested in.

This pleased me greatly. If my lucky streak in cathedrals held, we'd reach "Alabama" by nightfall. To our surprise, however, the first sight we saw was just as carnal—the Red Light District, where in addition to Surinamese women and bestiality magazines, cafes and bistros openly sell marijuana. Ever the eager travelers, we decided to sample the local cuisine. Ducking into a smoky little brown place, we found a menu of dope like a wine list. And since neither of us spoke Dutch, we ordered the only item listed in English: "Space Cake," also known as hash brownies.

We ate our first pieces in silence. Elapsed time: 30 minutes. I had completely forgotten that hash brownies take an hour to kick in. Since we didn't feel particularly stoned, we decided the stuff probably wasn't very potent. After all, how could it be? They sell it to tourists, for Pete's sake. If it was pungent, some idiots might accidentally eat too much, right?

Determined to get our money's worth, we ordered a second piece. Soon we were talking like we hadn't in years, as if we were a couple again. I mentioned "the Carolinas," and Mindy kissed me in a way that let me know she remembered that particular crime.

I had completely forgotten that when hash brownies kick in, they do so really hard. We started feeling pretty happy after our second pieces. Elapsed time: one hour. And so we decided, what the hell, let's have a third. I don't really remember much after that.

I remember noticing that when you're stoned, Dutch sounds a lot like English spoken by people from Wisconsin. And after that, there's a blank spot in my memory, a gap where the time is simply missing. And then I remember...suddenly noticing...that I was wiping my ass.

I wasn't sure how long I had been wiping my ass. But definitely I was wiping my ass. Probably for a long time. I noticed sitar music. Still I was wiping my ass. Evidently this was some sort of toilet place. How long I had been there, I did not know. I was relieved to learn I was wiping my ass in a toilet, and not somewhere else. The sitar didn't seem to be in the toilet with me. My ass seemed pretty sore. Possibly from all the wiping. The sitar music was nice, though.

And then: Where's Mindy?!

Panic-stricken and clinging to one frayed thread of awareness, I searched frantically for my pants. After several minutes, I found they had been conveniently placed around my ankles. I ventured out of the toilet, unsure of what I might find. I was in a restaurant.

It was an Indian restaurant. With really nice sitar music. I wasn't sure where the music was coming from. I didn't see a sitar anywhere. I also wasn't sure what I was looking for. The sitar music couldn't be coming from the toilet. That much was for sure. Mindy didn't even like Indian food. Surprising, then, that we would be in an Indian restaurant. Perhaps Mindy would know what I was looking...for...Mindy?!

Panic-stricken again, and still struggling for that one frayed thread of awareness, I desperately searched the room for Mindy. After an exhausting struggle, I discovered her approximately 2.5 feet to my left, giggling face-down in a pile of garlic naan. There was a tulip in her hair. Two down, I thought. And as a bonus, I was no longer wiping my ass.

There's another blank spot here. And then I remember: Mindy and I were suddenly sitting under a tree next to a canal with our arms around each other. We were scared. The high was getting more and more intense. Apparently we had decided to sit down and ride it out for as long as it lasted. We quietly rocked back and forth and murmured, "It's gonna be okay, it's gonna be okay...."

I looked up and realized we were sitting almost directly in front of the Anne Frank house. Tourists were watching us and pointing. Three for three, I thought. Mindy and I held each other tightly and looked into each other's eyes, knowing that, at least for a while, we needed each other desperately. It wasn't love, but it was certainly real.

A church bell struck noon. "It's gonna be okay, it's gonna be okay...." Before long, it was getting dark. My ass was way beyond numb from sitting on the pavement. The high was still peaking. We were still almost directly in front of the Anne Frank house.

I was convinced that by now everyone in Amsterdam knew we were stoned. Surely every tourist in Europe had heard about the fucked-up couple rocking and moaning in front of the Anne Frank house. Fodor's was rewriting their guidebook for Holland. Animals stared at us in dismay.

"It's gonna be okay, it's gonna be okay...."

There's another blank spot here, a long one. And then I remember: I awoke...as our train (huh?) rolled into a station. It was morning. We were in Berlin. Vividly I recall thinking, *Whoa!*

I took inventory. Finally, I was sober, at least as far as I could tell. Mindy was sound asleep in the next bunk. All of our things were packed and nearby. And we were in a sleeping compartment on a train. Entering Berlin.

Mindy didn't know why we were there, either. The prevailing theory is that we felt so guilty in our delirium for having disgraced the Anne Frank house that we sought the Nazi stronghold as penance. That's pure conjecture. If you can make up a better explanation, I'm all ears.

So Mindy and I wandered around Checkpoint Charlie (which is becoming a shopping mall) and the Brandenburg Gate (which is now an open-air market) and the weird giant onion-dome radio tower the Communists built (which now has a TGIFriday's across the street).

We tried all day to feel connected again, but Berlin is no damn place for young lovers. The romance was over. She got on a train for London that night. I never saw her again.

Thanks to Mindy, I'll never think of Ecuador or spend another Christmas Eve without feeling sad, and I'll never think of the states of the deep South without wistfully recalling a satisfied soreness in various obscure muscle groups.

I still have no idea what was in the Space Cake, and I know that the same neural overload that gave Mindy and me one last day of closeness also caused me to wipe my ass for perhaps an entire hour. But somehow it makes me happy to think of the whole ordeal this way: If Bogart and Bergman can always have Paris, then Mindy and I will always have Amsterdam.

Borderline Paranoia
Cat Simril Ishikawa

Driving through Europe with friend Jack in the summer of an earlier year. Jack was from a country that set new standards in straightness and I was just in from the land that Paul McCartney thought had legal weed. Fly, jailbird, fly. Neither of us had been stoned in ages. Then we got to the Netherlands. Rivers of hash. We ended up using it as a mosquito tranquilizer, and eventually had to leave.

Jack wanted to see Belgium. The guidebook said it was what you'd expect from a country with a national symbol of a boy pissing, but Jack insisted. He'd heard (quite rightfully) that it had the best beer in the world. But, of course, it was not the smoke utopia Netherlands, and we grew more and more worried as we neared the unknown land.

We sure tried to get rid of all our hash back in Amsterdam, but we still had a couple of orca-size joints under the seat. Jack was sure the border guards would find them. To smoke them would make us legally blind. What to do? I suspected Jack's worst nightmares weren't likely, but paranoia has a contagious quality, and it's better to be safe, insisted our jail-loathing consciences.

We spied a waste orb by the side of the road. Adieu, dear doobies, we said, and hurled them into the orb. Thanks for the Dutch treatment. Back in the car. We drive another few kilos through fields of small green things, and then we came to a store offering to change our money.

Change it into what, we wondered, and went inside. And discovered that we were already 10 km inside Belgium. There is no border. Between anything, after a while.

My Cannabis Cup Runneth Over
Paul Krassner

When Steve Hager, the editor of *High Times*, invited me to emcee the awards night at the 10th annual Cannabis Cup, I had to decline, regretfully, because I was committed to be in Detroit that week to cover the trial of Peter McWilliams, who has AIDS and cancer. He had been there for a family reunion and got arrested at the airport for possession of seven joints. Judge Tina Green said she would allow a medical marijuana defense, but one week later, she changed her mind.

That decision would be appealed, of course, and the trial was postponed, so I could fly to Amsterdam after all.

The Quentin Hotel, a friendly, funky place, was now filled entirely with Cannabis Cup attendees. In the lobby, folks were sitting around, drinking hot chocolate, talking, laughing and openly rolling, smoking and passing around huge doobies. I savored the culture shock.

In my tiny room, just around the corner from the lobby, there was a view of the canal and, right outside my window, a plain brick wall where someone had spray-painted the word SHIT in letters two feet high. Was this an omen or what?

Hager greeted me with a bud the size of a cucumber. Since all strains of marijuana at the Cannabis Cup have their own brand names—Purple Sage, White Shark, Stonehenge—I asked, "What's this one called?" He replied, "Dr. Kevorkian." I figured it would be killer weed. Actually, it cured my jet lag immediately. Yes, Dr. Kevorkian brought me back to life. It wasn't even entered in the competition, but it was already a winner.

In the lobby, a pot purist was pointing out that judges should avoid using a lighter when trying out a new brand, because the butane would taint the test. Rather, they should use a long wooden match, but wait until the sulfur is burned before lighting a joint. What about the glue on the rolling papers, I wondered. Someone offered me a cannabis cough drop. What a perfect concept. I sucked on it without missing a toke. And it worked; I didn't cough.

Over a period of five days, the judges would be trying out various kinds of pot grown by Amsterdam's top marijuana seed companies. They also traipsed around to a score of coffeeshops whose own brand names were in a separate competition. And, unlike at a wine-tasting event, these judges would not be spitting out each new sample.

At 4:20 each afternoon I went to the Council at Hemp Hall. There are different beliefs about the origin of 420 as a countercultural icon. One theory is that 420 is the police code for a pot bust. Another is that there are 420 substances in marijuana. Personally, I think that it comes from that old nursery rhyme about "four and twenty blackbirds." At home, I always light up promptly at 2:15 in the afternoon just to honor California's Proposition 215.

I hadn't expected, however, that 420 would also be celebrated in the lobby of the Quentin at 4:20 every *morning*. Drumming, singing, chanting, dancing, raucous conversation, loud giggles and wild guffaws would wake me up in the middle of the night. Naturally I would interpret that as a sign to select something from my stash and seize the opportunity to roll still another joint on *The New Testament*—printed in English and Hebrew, which surprised me. I thought that the Jewish people are still waiting for a messiah to appear for the first time. Jesus Christ, I was wrong again.

Ah, my ever-increasing stash. The seed companies and coffee-houses were giving out sample joints and little baggies of their product to all the judges, so it was a case of equal opportunity bribery. But, no matter how tempting, I would be afraid to bring any of it back to the States. Simply not worth the risk. At a *High Times* dinner, I sat next to Rita Marley and asked if she would be able to bring back any marijuana to Kingston. "No," she responded with a queenly air, adding, "Isn't it a pity?"

Joints were being passed around the table, but when I gestured to pass her one, she shook her head no. She was busy smoking a bomber of her own, which she didn't pass. I learned later that this is the practice in Jamaica. Apparently, there is no Rastafarian word for *bogart*.

My old Prankster friend Mountain Girl told me she was enter-taining the notion of buying a shovel and burying her gigantic stash. Next she thought of befriending a Dutch citizen and keeping it in his home. Or maybe she could obtain a safe-deposit box at the local bank—except that she'd have to open an account there first, and there wouldn't be time for a check to clear. She even consid-ered renting a small apartment in Amsterdam and living there for a couple of months until she had literally smoked herself out.

In my capacity as a stand-up satirist, I refrain from doing the comedy club circuit, which David Letterman calls "baby-sitting for drunks." Instead, I perform at alternative venues—from a New Age Expo to a Skeptical Inquirer Conference; from a Neo-Pagan Festival to a Swingers Convention—but I have never been at an event as joyful as the Cannabis Cup. I remain horrorstruck by the severe contrast between the drug laws of my own country and the ratio-nal approach I found in Amsterdam.

Before leaving, I climbed out the window of my hotel room and spray-painted on the brick wall so that the graffito would now read GOOD SHIT. At the airport in America, I experienced a moment of paranoia when I thought the narco-dog was about to sniff out *The New Testament* that I had borrowed from the hotel, but he passed by my luggage. *Whew!* The tension was almost worth the relief.

Now I was ready to return to cover Peter McWilliams' trial. The prosecutor in Detroit had legally changed his name to Luke Skywalker in 1977, when he was in his twenties and got inspired by *Star Wars*. He still goes by that name. Luke Skywalker battles medical marijuana. In court he will perceive McWilliams as Darth Vader. If this is justice, may the farce be with you.

Originally published in HIGH TIMES.

Chapter 17

Customs

Car Sale
Nancy Cain

During the mid-'70s I'm working with a company called Media Bus. We are funded through the New York State Council on the Arts and travel the state, teaching people how to make their own television shows and then taking them over to the local cable company to gain access.

One time, Media Bus is hired to stir things up a bit at the public access channel in Ann Arbor, Michigan. I make the trip with David, Carol and Skip. Carol is a little distracted because this is the first time she has left her daughter Sarah since she was born two years ago.

We're going to take the Canadian route instead of the Pennsylvania Turnpike. We'll drive up New York State and across Ontario to Detroit. Then we can stay with my mom and dad, and drive out to Ann Arbor in the morning. Relaxed, no-traffic country roads all the way. Idyllic day, at least for me, just riding along incommunicado, as if free.

Canada has a different vibe. A slower beat. After a while I relax and stop thinking that we're going to get pulled over by the cops at any moment, like I do when we're on the New York Thruway, for example. A sunny, happy day away. That is, until US Customs. That's the price you pay for taking the scenic route. You have to go through US Customs.

Always a complex and dangerous game.

Sometimes it's not paranoia. Sometimes it's intuition. Sometimes you just know when your number is up. That's the way I feel when I see that the Customs inspector moving toward me is a woman. She escorts me alone through a door into a small anteroom.

The officers have already ripped our car apart and taken our video reels out of the boxes and held the tape up to the light. They have already taken out the back seat, and they say, "Found a seed." Jesus. A seed. Maybe they did. Shit.

Oh, they would have stopped us anyway, because we fit a profile. Skip with his thick blond hair flowing way down his back, and David with his black beard out to there—Carol and I are not exactly in business suits either—and, well, I guess we do seem like a suspicious bunch.

The Customs inspector is closing the door behind her. She stares at me. Dry mouth. Heart palpitations. Mine, not hers. The little leather pouch of pot is burning a hole in my shirt pocket. I am a guilty murderer.

"You'd better give it to me, because if I find it, it's gonna be way worse."

I hear the squish-squish of my blood pumping past my eardrums. Poomb! Poomb! My heart. I examine my options and hand over the pot. And I keep my mouth shut. Now she wants me to strip and squat to make sure I don't have anything else stashed up inside me. Gee, this is happening to me and I'm not dying. Hey, it's just a little dignity. Take it.

Turns out they searched Skip and David and Carol too, but they were clean. Now the four of us are sitting on a hard bench, waiting for the Customs inspectors to come up with the next scenario. Here they come. The deal is that we are guilty of bringing a controlled substance across an international border in a vehicle, and the United States government consequently is going to take ownership of our vehicle.

"Wait a minute," Skip says incredulously. "You mean that the government now owns our car?"

Yes, it's true. That's the bad news. The good news is that we can buy it back from them for only $100. Wow! Really? Because this is a brand new 1973 Dodge Dart four-door. Same color green as the phone company's cars. A hundred dollars is a bargain. We buy it (leaving us with maybe $30 between us) and are kicked unceremoniously out onto Jefferson Avenue, Detroit, Michigan, USA.

It's nighttime. We arrive at my mom and dad's late, and we're all excited about our border experience, which we relate breathlessly, leaving out the part where they find my pot.

Producing our live video-chaos television show in Ann Arbor is as bizarre and controversial as ever, but nothing tops US customs for a thrill.

Excerpted from the memoir, *The Beginner.*

Lobsters
Dan Denov

It was sometime in the winter of 1971-72 and we were in the home stretch of a jaunt to New York and Boston, a mere couple of hours to Lansing, Michigan. To save time we cut across Canada from Niagara Falls toward Windsor/Detroit. Somewhere in that stretch, we had pulled off the highway to get a cup of coffee, take a leak and stretch,.

While searching in this small town for the way back to the highway, we picked up a cop who threw the lights on and pulled us over. He said it looked like we were lost—white VW bus, Illinois plates and three somewhat unkempt guys at 9 o'clock that night. We said yes and he showed us the way out of town. Nice country, that Canada. Anyway, our stash of an ounce or so wasn't even close to an issue at this point. Onward to the border.

In due time we made it out of Canada at Windsor, over the bridge and on to Customs in the US. It was so easy to get into and out of Canada, we anticipated an easy re-entry to the good old USA, but just for safekeeping we stashed the pot down one of our pants. It was now around two in the morning. A youngish guy in a uniform came over, asked me details of where, when and why, and then proceeded to look at the two pretending to be asleep in the back with that haze of road buzz about them. He asked us to step out and into the Customs house. We, at that point, were starting to worry a bit, and that worry quickly expanded when the young guy came in and said he'd "found some seeds" in the car and that everything needed to be searched.

We had all the usual paraphernalia for a road trip—sleeping bags, fast food containers, eight-track wired into the dome light in the back and a supply of Firesign Theater, Doors and Jimi Hendrix tapes—but we had also picked up, at one of our compatriot's request, some live lobsters in Boston to bring home. Amongst all our bags and boxes of crap now in the Customs house, the guards proceeded to empty the cooler box, at which point the two lobsters started crawling around on the stainless steel countertop.

The officer must have figured that there were "bigger fish to fry" and corralled the clawed creatures back into their temporary home. Not finding much of anything in all the stuff they hauled out of the bus, they proceeded to strip-search us one at a time in the bathroom. I forget the order in which we went, but I do remember what the oldest of the officers said to me as owner of the vehicle when they found the stashed stash: "Son, you're in a lot of trouble."

It came down to this—I had an hour to come up with $150 or, in their words, they'd tear my bus apart. At first I thought it was a bribe, but figured out later, after looking at the official receipt I have to this day, that the only federal law concerning marijuana was an importation tax of $100 an ounce! I was busted for trying to smuggle the stuff in without paying the tax. Of course this revelation didn't help in terms of the money at 4:30 a.m. A good college buddy of mine was living in Detroit at his folks' house, so I gave him a call. His mother answered the phone and, although she mainly spoke Ukrainian, understood what I was saying and put Head on the line. I quickly reeled off the scenario and he said he'd be right down.

Now this guy is about 6'5" and around 250 pounds and at the time was selling phone systems for AT&T in the Detroit area. When he walked into the Customs house clean-shaven and in his three-piece suit, put his attaché case on the counter and clicked it open, the officers weren't quite sure what was happening. When he said, with a glance toward us—"What kind of trouble my boys in?"—their jaws seemed to come down a little slack. I told the Head to give them $150, which he peeled off a small wad. They wrote a receipt, and we were out the door to a doughnut shop (sans the dope). Those guards must have figured they had run into some connected freaks for us to have gotten that kind of response with one phone call at 4:30 in the morning.

Got One!
Kathleen Edwards

Two carefree people taking a casual tour of the northern United States, we opted for a detour into Canada. Never been there. Wanted to see what it was like. We thought it might be a good rehearsal for our impending year-long trip through Europe.

The Border Patrol on the US side of the Canadian border at Sault Ste. Marie took one look at the 1968 Volkswagen van with bicycles on top, California plates and a long-haired, bearded driver, and their eyes lit up. You could see them mentally rubbing their hands together. "Boy, this is gonna be fun."

"Get out of the van and step inside." Since we had finished off the last of the half-pint of whiskey the previous evening and we were sure the van was "clean," we faced this challenge casually. We were escorted into a dreary room with a handful of potbellied, ruddy-faced career cops. "Wait right here." We watched as a pair of these cops ambled toward the van.

A few minutes passed, then the "searchers" returned. In their stubby hands, they held what appeared to be a short, fat roach. We looked at each other's eyes and what passed silently between us was, "Where did that come from?" Although we are admittedly partakers of the herb, this roach didn't resemble anything we'd ever seen.

They then explained that this roach was to be dropped into a solution and, if it turned purple, that would prove it was cannabis. They stood around like Einstein-wannabes and indeed the solution did change to a purple haze. One cop rushed to a telephone, pushed a couple of buttons and proudly shouted, "Got one!" We surmised that they kept a supply of these roaches around as an excuse to search any "suspicious persons."

Since they were going to search the van, they would, of course, find it necessary to search our persons. While waiting for a female officer to arrive (45 minutes later), these protectors of our borders methodically went through every corner of the van. They were itching to get us on something. They even went so far as to count our traveler's checks because, as was explained to us later, it is illegal to carry more than $5,000 across the Canadian border. Imagine their disappointment when they found only $3,800.

As for the strip search, that has to be pretty high up there on the humiliation scale. The female officer was curt but judgmental. "You must have had something for them to call on me to search you."

Through this entire scene, my partner and I never spoke to one another, but merely knowingly nodded. Surprisingly, since they found nothing in the van, they unceremoniously handed us the keys without a word of acknowledgment or apology, and went back to their doughnuts. The lesson here is simple. We were about to embark on a journey through foreign countries, yet we endured an experience within our own borders which evoked visions of *Midnight Express*.

The story itself is really the middle of a longer story which has a beginning story and end story to it.

The beginning of the story involved being turned away from the Canadian border by the authorities there because my partner and I answered their questionnaire with complete honesty and he said that he had been arrested as a teenager for marijuana possession. They refused our entry and turned us back to the US, which initially explains the actions of the US Border Patrol. We suspect they received a phone call.

The end of this story involves the same VW van and two hits of LSD. All I can say about this is, if you want to put something somewhere no one will find it, try the inside of a Tampax box. I'm willing to bet that there's no male officer out there who'd put his hand inside such a box, even though the contents are cleanly wrapped and unused.

Pleasant Surprise?

Back in the late 1960s and early 1970s, hitchhiking was part of the culture for hippies. I learned to hitchhike when I visited my sister in San Francisco for two weeks. Hitching was more than a means of transportation. It was an expression of communalism—those who had transportation would share with those who didn't. I was living in Chicago, and I soon made it a practice to hitch a ride down Halsted Street to get to school rather than take the bus.

It was sometime around 1971 when my friend Steve and I decided to hitch to Toronto to visit a friend who was dodging the draft. Someone with more hitching experience than us had advised us not to accept a ride to Gary, Indiana. He said you could get a ride very easily with someone going to work at the steel mill there, but it would be hard to get another ride from that point. Far better to turn down 10 rides to Gary and wait for a car that was traveling further.

We started out early in the morning, and within five minutes a car stopped and the driver offered us a ride to Gary. We shrugged our shoulders and got in. Boy, that was easy! By late afternoon, we were still in Gary. We had progressed from the west side of Gary to the east side. But we were still a whole lot closer to Chicago than we were to Toronto. The sun was beating down on us. We were tired and sweaty and talking about giving up and hitching a ride back home to Chicago. Hitchhiking was supposed to be fun, but this was discouraging.

Finally, a van full of hippies stopped to pick us up. They said they were going as far as London, Ontario. It was a stroke of luck. Better yet, they had a bag full of dope. After a couple of joints, all of the day's earlier frustrations were forgotten. The music sounded good, we were having good conversation with some good people, and everything was mellow. We got to Detroit and were about to cross over into Canada when we realized our dilemma. We can't cross the border with a bag of dope. The Customs agents might search the vehicle and arrest us. But it would be an awful shame to waste a bag of good weed. What should we do?

Someone got the idea that we should drive around and look for a hippie to give it to, so it wouldn't be wasted (better that the hippie should be wasted than the dope). We drove around for 10 minutes, knowing nothing about the neighborhood. We saw Tiger Stadium, we saw some policemen, but we didn't see any hippies. Okay, let's go into a restaurant, get a snack, and maybe we'll find a hippie in there. There were a couple of tables occupied by cops, but no hippies.

We got back in the van. We were determined to give this weed away to someone who would appreciate it before we crossed the border. We drove around some more, but we had no luck. Finally, we stopped beside a parked car with an open window, dropped the bag of dope on the seat, and took our chances. We laughed at the possibility that some totally straight person would discover it. We hoped some happy freak would discover it and that we would make his day.

As it turned out, the Customs agent didn't search the van. He just asked the driver a few questions and waved us on through. We could have kept the bag in the van and smoked a few more joints. But then I wouldn't be able to contribute this story to Paul Krassner's book. Of course, we have no idea how the story ended. I've often wondered about it in the ensuing years. I can hope for the best, but I can also think of some rather unpleasant scenarios:

1. A mother and her teenage son return to the car, and she screams, "Junior! What in the world are you doing with this?"

2. A couple on their first date return to the car, and she says, "Philip, you said you didn't do drugs."

3. A paranoid freak discovers it. He wants to smoke it, but he thinks it's been planted by the cops.

4. An undercover cop returns to his car, and uses the bag of weed to plant at an apartment he wants to bust.

I guess we'll never know. We were just trying to give someone a pleasant surprise. I hope we did.

Spanish Lie
Bob Wieder

In 1970 I was returning to Spain from Morocco. Spain was then notorious for its draconian attitude toward drugs. I had everything I owned stuffed in a massive duffel bag. "Everything" included some kif that was really too valuable and salubrious to leave behind, and a bunch of long wooden carved pipe stems and clay and sandstone pipe bowls, which to this day I find the optimal vehicles for pot-smoking.

The people I was traveling with had all left their illicit goods behind, but I put my remaining kif at the very bottom of my duffel bag, and all the pipe stuff right on the top. The general opinion was that I would wind up learning a lot of Spanish over the next 10-15 years.

At Spanish Customs (off the ferry from Tangiers), an inspector opened my bags, saw the pipes and did a whopping double-take.

"What is this?" he asked.

"Those are pipes," I said.

"For what?" he asked.

"For smoking."

"For smoking what?" he inquired knowingly.

"For smoking marijuana back in the USA," I said.

He gave me his Aha look: "You have the marijuana in the bag too, right?"

I gave him my don't-be-ridiculous look: "Are you kidding? I'd go to jail! Everybody knows that Spanish Customs is the toughest in the world. I want the pipes to use back home, but I knew I'd never be able to sneak them past you. That's why I put them right on top, to just get it out of the way. But come on, I'd be nuts to put hash pipes where a Spanish Customs officer could see them if I was carrying drugs. Nobody fools you guys!"

He gave me an eminently pleased smile and waved me in.

Divine Intervention
Celina Herrero

I was on the second leg of a three-day trans-Mexico odyssey—a 48-hour bus ride from Tijuana to Mexico City. Two friends had driven me across the border and, as carrying drugs into Mexico from the States is rarely an issue, I had a quarter-ounce of fragrant, potent skunk bud in a clear plastic sandwich bag ever-so-carelessly tossed into an upper side pocket of my camping backpack together with several pairs of rolled-up socks. Not cleverly tucked inside a pair of socks, mind you, nothing that prudent; rather just sitting there where it would be immediately visible to anyone who happened to unzip that particular pocket.

I was sleeping soundly, as we veteran travelers tend to do on long, tedious bus journeys, snoring away as our "luxury coach" sped through the star-infested nightscape of the endless desert, a nothingness broken only by scattered stumpy cacti and a few frolicking nocturnal jackrabbits. Suddenly, heart-stoppingly, the bus came to an abrupt halt outside an ominously official-looking building in the middle of nowhere, a hideous squat concrete hut crouching malevolently in the night.

Several uniformed officers invaded the bus and immediately began pulling luggage off the overhead racks, shouting in Spanish: "Customs! Everybody off the bus! Let's go, baggage, suitcases, everything, let's go, keep it moving." They swaggered up and down the aisle—half a dozen of them, at least—banging suitcases about and roughly shaking people awake in that endearing, people-person manner in which law-enforcement officers the world over seem to have been specially trained. One minute I'd been dreaming of my upcoming month in a hammock under a palm tree in a Caribbean utopia, the next I was facing cops, all kinds of unpleasantness (or am I being redundant?) and, barring divine intervention, some serious time in jail. Mexican jail.

They were everywhere all at once, leaving no window of opportunity in which to surreptitiously dump the bag of weed onto the floor of the bus or take any other ass-saving measures whatsoever. Under the watchful eye of a veritable army of Customs officers, every last passenger, blinking and groggy, dragging along pieces of baggage, was prodded and shoved into the Customs dungeon.

The place was enormous, with some 20 different stations, each consisting of a long concrete table on which to have a proper snoop through our belongings, and staffed by a series of weary-eyed, heavy-set older women who looked wet behind the ears. As we waited in a single line for the next available life-wrecker, I with a knot in my gut the size of Jalisco sent out a fervent prayer to the universe: "Please, God, the young guy. Please, God, the young guy." I chanted this silently over and over, a heartfelt, desperate, I-don't-want-to-go-to-jail-in-Mexico mantra.

Happily, my prayers were answered. To my great relief, when my turn came I was spared the fate of dealing with the grouchy grandmas and was sent instead to the lone young guy for my baggage check. I relaxed slightly at this point, taking it as a sign that, for the moment anyway, God, or someone with considerable cosmic pull, was on my side. If only my luck would hold.

The young man, predictably enough, was friendly and curious and made casual flirty small talk with me as he (gulp!) began to very thoroughly inspect the contents of my bag. He opened every lipstick, leafed through every magazine, took every cassette out of its box, felt up the padded collar of my winter jacket, and poked a finger into the coin pocket of my jeans (destroying any hope I had that they might be looking only for guns).

By this point, I was kicking myself for actually requesting this earnest, out-to-prove-something, takes-his-job-way-too-seriously young go-getter. Maybe I would have been better off after all with one of the bad-humored old ladies, who probably just wanted to get it over with and go back to their siestas. Maybe he was prolonging the search in order to continue flirting with me a little longer. In any case, I was stuck with him, and I played the eyelash-batting, flattering gringo señorita role for all it was worth.

He was full of questions. "Your Spanish is so good, señorita. Where did you learn to speak it so well?" "How long will you be staying in Mexico?" "What is your final destination?" I chatted his ear off, prattling nervously away about my previous trips to the Yucatan, how much I loved the southern part of the country, how open and friendly I found the Mexican people.

The young cop was conducting a painfully thorough counterclockwise tour of every nook, cranny and crevice of my huge overstuffed rucksack, and behind my bright-eyed, beaming flirtatiousness I was hopeless. No one searching that thoroughly could possibly miss a big, stinky clump of sticky, hairy buds in a clear plastic bag. After all, no attempt had been made to camouflage or hide it in any way; it just nestled in among the rolled-up socks in plain view inside what would be the last pocket to be searched, silently screaming, "Bust me!" In my imagination, I had already fast-forwarded to my years in prison. Would it be as bad as I thought? How much time would they give me? Would I finally get that novel written?

Cop-boy had by this time gotten to the toiletries and cosmetics pouch, which would be the second-to-last pocket to be inspected on his counterclockwise search of my belongings. Last (but by no means least) would be, of course, the "socks and controlled sub-

stances" compartment. He began rummaging through my most
personal items, pulling out shampoo, vitamins, a toothbrush—and
condoms. Lots of them.

Before embarking on this journey, I had found myself enduring
a flurry of last-minute get-togethers with friends and family members. Though I was only planning to be gone for a month, girl-
friends, my sister and my mother all insisted, "Let's meet for a
drink before you leave. I have a little going-away present for you."

By some hilarious "coincidence," the going-away gift was in
each case the same: condoms. Boxes of condoms, loose condoms,
ribbed, extra-sheer, flavored condoms (chocolate, grape, jalapeño,
molé), industrial-strength condoms, lubricated condoms, condoms
in a variety of colors (red, blue, green, purple) and a variety of
sizes (small, medium and ay, caramba). I had thought it so funny
that so many different people had seen fit to give me condoms for
my south-of-the-border adventure that at the last minute I tossed
every last one of them into a gallon-size plastic freezer bag and
brought them along. There must have been 80 or 90 condoms altogether.

I was sweating by this point, as the sole remaining pocket to be
searched contained my one-way ticket to Sonora State Prison. I
trembled and breathed deeply and tried to savor my last few seconds of sweet freedom. I had forgotten about the condoms—at
least, forgotten how many there were, how varied and colorful
and downright impressive they looked in the huge clear bag. The
young officer's eyes grew wide and he stammered slightly as,
incredulous, he repeated one of his earlier questions to me.

"Uh, how long did you say you were planning to stay in Mexico
again?"

"About three weeks," I replied, smiling sweetly.

He blanched visibly. Holding the bag gingerly between thumb
and forefinger as if afraid that mere contact with that many condoms might somehow infect him with some life-threatening disease, he carefully replaced the bag and toiletries case in the pocket, zipped it closed and pushed the backpack over to me with a
grin and a leer.

"Have a wonderful time in our country, señorita."

Chapter 18

Varieties of Paranoia

Lapse in Judgment
Hunter Thompson

I have always loved marijuana. It has been a source of joy and comfort to me for many years. And I still think of it as a basic staple of life, along with beer and ice and grapefruit—and millions of Americans agree with me.

I've always been quite moderate with my use of marijuana except for eating it, which has caused a lot of trouble—overindulging in brownies, eating hash. Those are some of the worst physical reactions I've ever had. Being in someone else's car in some strange neighborhood. Not being able to get a cigarette out of your pocket, horrible cold sweats, unable to talk, thinking you're yelling for help and just whispering—praying for death, really.

I was in Zaire during the Ali-Foreman fight and everyone was smoking this black, grainy, East African weed. It was utterly paralyzing, terrifying weed, not necessarily hallucinogenic. It was more like running into a closed door. You think it's open, you start walking through and bash your head into an oaken slab. It could put a room full of people into a coma, one by one. I smoked it all the time—huge spliffs—went a little psychotic, overtones of everything.

I became convinced I should eat all my malaria pills which were supposed to be eaten once a week on Tuesday. Very powerful orange things. The doctor assured me he didn't mean Wednesday or Monday, that it was important I follow the prescribed dosage.

I had this conversation with a guy named Big Black, a conga drummer. We got to know each other pretty well. Big Black knew a lot more about malaria pills than I did. He had white ones that he took once a day. So, I said, what the hell, and began eating my pills just like Big Black. I didn't have that many, but I had enough to give myself malaria—a real psychotic episode. I went absolutely crazy. I lost about three or four days wandering around Zaire.

Hide and Seek
Gerri Willinger

I walked in the door, and crashed on the couch after a three-hour night class at the University of Wisconsin in Milwaukee. I always kept my stash on the coffee table.

I was laying on the couch, and heard a knock on the door. Mom opened it. I heard, "FBI, ma'am, can we use your phone?" I could hear my mom laughing as she walked past me, tossing a blanket over me (my head and torso mostly) as though it were a natural thing to do, as she led them to the phone. She just said, "She had a hard day at school."

I had a wolfhound who was not pleased with my lying stiff as a board and only two legs showing. She had the personality of Catherine the Great (or any other empress) and decided to jump on me with her five-foot-tall body and act as though I were a trampoline. That was her way of letting me know she was displeased. She did this the entire time the FBI agents were there.

There I was being used as a trampoline by an imperial dog while the FBI is calling in to headquarters because they had lost the address of the house they were supposed to bust and they did not want any bad publicity.

I was under the cover with my eyes opened wide enough to roll out of my head, pretending to sleep, as these very polite men apologized for bothering us. As I was about to have a heart attack, I wondered what they were thinking of my mom's giggling.

When they left, I immediately went for my stash and rolled a big one.

Vega
Mr. Howell

Do you remember the Chevrolet Vega? It came in a number of versions and was the Big Three car companies' response to rising gasoline prices in the early '70s. I owned this station-wagon version. Compared to the true station wagons of the era like Ford's monolithic Country Squire, it was a true miniature and intended, I suppose, to confuse anyone thinking about buying something foreign-made. You could still pack a lot of stuff in a Vega wagon. Everything I owned could fit in it and still leave room in the front passenger seat for my dog. Her name, of course, was Vega.

Vega is an okay name for a dog, and it gave me one less thing to remember. I was doing a very short tour of duty in the Army at the time, and living in the enlisted barracks at a fort in Georgia. We were all young and very glad we were not going to Vietnam. The US Army was in a state of shock, Tricky Dick had been canned, our current commander-in-chief apparently couldn't climb stairs without injuring himself, and we were left to do pretty much as we pleased.

We partied a lot. Even right in the barracks. Guys were rotating back from Asia who had actually been shot at, and—when the Army felt they had decompressed enough—began joining us in the regular barracks. These people were so glad to be alive—reprieved from death at the hands of an enemy most of them never even saw—that no amount of debauchery or intoxication was too much. But, God, we tried.

Pretty soon we ran out of dope. In fact, the whole base went dry, and it was time for a logistical resupply mission of some magnitude. This would turn out to be the only mission of any merit that I would ever be sent on, so I took two weeks leave and headed south. My orders: Score four pounds of the best pot I could find.

With Vega next to me in the passenger seat, it was nice to be on the road. The two weeks went by, and I was headed back to station with the shopping list filled and a case of real Mexican-made Kahlua to boot. I was on US Highway 1 North, and just passing through many small rural communities that populate its roadside, when the blue and red lights of a municipal police car slashed across my rear-view mirror.

Bummer, adrenaline, life flashes. Can you say *Midnight Express*, y'all? The Georgia correctional system was not perceived as a positive life experience, judging from the ever-present roadside gangs. I didn't look good in stripes, can't eat fifty eggs in one sitting, and people with mirror sunglasses and shotguns make me uncomfortable.

I pulled to the side of the road and looked at Vega. Dogs can sense when you are scared shitless. My ears were ringing with fear when I heard a voice say, "Let me see your license and registration, son. You were doin' thirty-seven in a twenty-five zone back there." I pulled my wallet and fished the other papers out of the glove compartment. I had everything in my right hand and was reaching across my chest to hand over the papers when Vega struck.

In an instant, she had hold of the constable's blue jacket sleeve, and there was considerable growling and cursing. As I pulled her away from the window, the jacket sleeve gave way with a loud— really loud—ripping noise. With my right hand on top of Vega, I reached out in vain to hand over my papers. All I could see of the policeman's face was my own reflection in the mirror aviator frames and a frown that looked extremely pissed off.

"All right, boy, follow me to the station."

I did as he asked, of course. We pulled into the gravel and red-clay parking area with the lights of the police car still flashing. He didn't even look at me, just waved his hand as he trudged into the building. I followed him into the building, and he was already seated with the offended jacket lying on the desk in front of him. I was shaking like a leaf while he stared at my driver's license, and we waited for a call back on whether I had any outstanding warrants.

Everything came back clear.

"You ready to pay the fine now, son, an' you can go. You're a serviceman so that's all I'm gonna do. That'll be thuty-seven dol-lahs—cash."

I about pissed myself walking out of that building. Vega seemed pleased to see me as well.

Bank Job
Judita

Pam and I were on our way to the desert when we realized neither of us had any pot. We called around, and the only person we could get was the man who sold "tea." You ordered it by code, and I even had my own pin number.

We were on our way out of town, so it was decided we would meet Jack on the off-ramp of Lincoln Boulevard at the gas station. When he arrived, he told us that the pot was still wet, so spread it out and let it dry.

We were in too much of a hurry to wait, so we took our first hit immediately, and we were off to the bank to replenish our funds. When we arrived at the bank, Pam decided to stay in the car and let the motor run so she could use the heater to dry the stuff.

I went into the bank and immediately felt there was something wrong, but I was very stoned, so at first I thought it was my imagination. I got into line and noticed that everyone seemed to be standing still.

I waited a few moments and still no one moved, so finally I got up my courage and turned around and called to the manager, "What's wrong—is this a hold-up?"

As I said this, it unfroze everyone, and the robber ran right by me out into the street. I realized that Pam was in danger with the car motor running, parked right in front of the bank, and all that pot in her lap. Paradise for anyone.

As I ran out toward Pam, the police and guards gave chase after the robber. I jumped into my car with the motor still running, hoping the police would not mistake me for the thief. They didn't, and we were off onto another adventure....

Stems and Seeds

A poor little rich boy that I worked with, "Joe College," asked me to score a quarter-pound of pot for him to take back to school. As usual, the late summer dry spell was upon us and pot was scarce. I had heard that this guy across the street had been busted a couple of years before for coke so I thought maybe he still had some connections.

We sat on my front steps shooting the shit for a while, and then he told me to stop over later and he'd have the pot for me. When he let me into his apartment there were a half dozen or so guys sitting around. I was probably stoned and didn't pay much attention to them, but I was taken aback a bit when he handed me the quarter-pound out in the middle of the room in front of everybody.

But I thought he was cool so I assumed the rest of the guys were too, or he wouldn't be conducting business in front of them. I took the pot home and after a while Joe College came over to check it out. Like I said, we were in a dry spell, but Joe was picky and didn't want the pot. Too many stems and seeds.

Oh, well, it was fronted to me so I'd just take it back. As I was getting ready to walk out the door a while later to do just that, someone knocked on the door. I didn't know the guy but I recognized him. He hung out at the same bar my friends and I went to every weekend. It was a dive bar that we sat around in smoking joints. It was paradise, soon to be a parking lot.

He said he was from "John's" across the street and was wondering what was up with the quarter-pound. I told him I was just on my way back over with the pot because my friend wasn't satisfied with the quality and we hadn't smoked any. I gave it back to him and he left.

Some weeks later, after Joe College had gone back to school and paradise had been razed, I was telling a girl at work who knew John about the whole incident. "After John got busted," she tells me, "he turned narc to stay out of prison." What?

It all became clear then. The crowd in John's apartment, the guy popping in with the excuse he was concerned about the pot when he was really trying to see who I was getting it for, and the bar where no one hassled us about smoking joints. Hell, Big Brother was probably watching us the whole time! I was sure glad then that Joe College hadn't wanted the pot. He would've been looking through books and I would have been looking through bars.

Radical Luck
Tom Craig

It was early spring, 1971. I, my wife and young child, along with two fellow students, shared a house in a working-class suburb of Washington, DC. We had all moved in together after leaving/being-asked-to-leave the major radical commune of our university because of a perceived lack of proper revolutionary spirit. It was the wild and woolly times of the Revolution.

Even our staid old preppy college, Georgetown University, had risen up the previous spring after the invasion of Cambodia and Kent State and "Shut it down," and even that fall there had been a local version of "Days of Rage" in the streets of trendy old Georgetown, which required a massive mobilization of DC cops to restore order.

Our two roommates, Steve and Ray, were wildly wacky anarchistic dope dealers who, about every two weeks, had a well-dressed visitor from California fly in and deliver a large suitcase full of Acapulco Gold and other goodies for local distribution. Needless to say, our house was unique on our little side street, where office workers and tradespeople left early in the morning, lunches packed, to pursue their version of the American dream.

We even had a Virginia State Trooper living about five doors down, who parked his patrol car out in front of the house. It was a living reminder of where we were, if not in the belly, at least in the gullet of the Beast. For the most part we were fairly discreet, but after one large shipment from the Golden State, we planned our first big party. The May Day demonstrations of that year were winding down, and there was major steam that needed to be released.

Ray, the trickster of the dynamic duo, organized a gathering of our fellow art class students, assorted radicals and hippies, and even some of the Vietnam Vets Against the War from around the country who had trekked to Washington and whom we had brought out from their encampment down on the Mall.

Steve, not to be outdone, invited his band down from Long Island to provide musical accompaniment for the spectacle. So here we were in a small two-story house in sleepy little Falls Church, Virginia, with a loud band wailing in the basement and about 40 stoned people sipping Boone's Farm. Soon the sickly sweet smell of righteous herb seemed to be wafting from the very heating ducts themselves.

I had always been the "father figure" of the household. Everything was in my name, and I fixed the clogged sinks, etc., so naturally I was feeling a little paranoid and responsible. I remember even going out in the front yard to check the noise and hilarity level, which much to my surprise was relatively under control. Finally I decided to abandon myself to the revelry and proceeded to compete in the shotgun and bong events with great relish. After my consciousness had been significantly altered, I drifted into a relaxed state and began having a marvelous time.

I thought our little house had been successfully launched into an orbit around Jupiter and was far beyond the clutches of the sad violent gray world it had once stood in. Somewhere along that time, I heard someone calling my name loudly from a distance. I swam down through the haze and wandered toward the front door where I saw Ray, grinning widely to someone outside and motioning me to come and deal with these new guests, just hidden from my sight behind the opened door.

All right, Ray, I thought, what is waiting for me, a face-painted ghoul, a naked lady, a pie in the face? Ray, still beaming, stepped back to get a better look at my facial reaction as I came around the door. There on our doorstep stood two fresh-faced, red-cheeked Virginia troopers, grinning almost as beneficently as Ray. I swallowed hard, smiled weakly and tried to ignore the wafting ganja smoke escaping from the upper doorway.

"Can I help you?" I managed to ask. Still grinning, one of the troopers addressed me in a broad cracker drawl: "We were just passing by and we noticed that one of the doors on that red van was open, and it being after midnight and all, we wanted to make sure everything was okay." I jumped at the chance to go inspect and lead them away from the smoking house, thanking them profusely.

Next day as I was leaving for town, I saw a State Police car rounding the bend in front of our house. The driver wore the same grin he had had last night as he waved cheerfully to me, happy to greet his new neighbor. Was he a nice guy, just doing his job? A curious but benign straight hoping to catch some orgy scene? Or a good ole boy just a-messin' with our minds? Damned if I know. I'm just glad I kept my underwear clean that night.

Foolish Question
Jerry Ochs

In the early '70s I shared a house with seven other people—some college students, some married working couples. We liked to smoke pot and there was always some around except for one horrible day when we realized that we all had run dry at the same time.

Everyone being conscientious communalists, each person made an extra effort that day to score, and at dinnertime the results spoke for themselves. A kilo here and a half-kilo there and minimountains of pot in front of each person.

In order to judge the quality of this cornucopia of maryjane, each person rolled one joint from their stuff and we smoked them one at a time. At about the time we were toking on contestant number five, which had reached the status of roach, there was an abrupt and violent knocking at the front door.

Bob, the nervous type, holding the roach and sitting at a table piled high with pot, eyes wide with fear, squeaked, "Should I swallow it?"

Chapter 19

Not Busted

These Untidy Guys
Michelle Phillips

Our rented car with almost all our worldly possessions had been stolen from the underground car park on Franklin. We reported it to the police and, in the pace of events, forgot about it.

After moving to Flores, we had a visit without warning from a member of the FBI. The car had been found and had been stolen by someone they were interested in. I invited him in and he began to spell out his story, while I, horrified, froze.

All across the coffee table was an array of marijuana in various stages of preparation and cleaning: a hundred joints, all neatly rolled, separated and stacked by Denny. Buds still clinging together from the fields, some cleaned, some twigs, a lot of seeds. A whole mess of pot.

While the FBI agent told his tale of sleuthing rewarded, I decided that the only way to deal with this awful sideshow of cannabis was to busy myself like a housewife. I took a big paper bag from the market and started shoving all the marijuana into it, all the while playing the scene as if to say: "These untidy guys around here—always leaving things around."

If the FBI man knew or suspected anything, he never indicated it to me. His eyes didn't stray to the table. He just kept to the subject at hand—the stolen car—while I showed suitable interest: "Really? How amazing! Well, now. Gee!"

The Hole-in-the-Floor Gang

A whole bunch of us jumped into my friend's van to go to Starved Rock, Illinois. For the 14 of us we took three ounces of high-grade weed. After spending several hours there and getting very stoned, we started back. For some reason that made perfect sense then, we decided to travel down one of the main streets of town.

Suddenly the driver said that the cops were right behind us and wanted to pull us over. Underneath the carpeting on the floor was a big hole that had once been part of the frame but was now surrounded with rust. Out that hole went pipes, papers, roach clips and, in three different baggies, an ounce-and-a-half of smoke.

The cops stopped and searched each of us, the males much more thoroughly than the females, but we were all lucky that we had dumped our stashes. We had to follow the squad car to the cop shop where they gave the driver a bogus ticket—why didn't they do that on the spot?—and told us to get out of town. They were not amused when we pointed out to them that we already would be if they hadn't made us go to the station.

We went back to see if we could find any of our stash as most of us figured that we needed a smoke. We were able to find two pipes, one roach clip, one partial pack of papers and about half an ounce of weed. After going over the drop zone twice, we left town fast.

About a month after the incident, I was helping the van owner replace the muffler. Stuck in the frame just "downwind" of the hole we found a bag of dope. We figured that we should forget the muffler and in honor of our trip to Starved Rock we should smoke the dope.

We started to, and his brother and a friend arrived home to help us. When they heard the story, we turned it into a religious ceremony and got totally stoned.

The Grateful Living
Woody

On a typical Saturday evening around 11 p.m., me and some friends decided to go to the cemetery just to smoke and be with the dead. (Don't worry, we're not vampires or anything.) We hopped over the fence surrounding the burial ground and lit up a huge joint. We went to the back to lay down on the hill. We had brought along some more weed 'cause we do smoke too much.

This cemetery being close to the highway, somebody must have seen us and called the cops. Flashlights were seen coming from afar, but we thought nothing of it, assuming more friends were on their way. Hell, no! The cops said that if we wanted to smoke, to do it in a safe place, not in public like that.

As we were exiting the place, we had to walk alongside the highway to return to our homes, and they passed by us with their sirens on, yelling over the intercom, "Yabba dabba doo," over and over again as they vanished in the fog.

Nickel Bag

Back in 1964, on a hot summer day in New York, my friend Mitch and I (17 years old) were in his '52 Desoto going the wrong way down a one-way street under the old West Side Highway. We were stopped by cops who found the joint that Mitch couldn't ditch in time but didn't find the one I tossed under the parked car.

We had discovered a method of grinding up peyote buttons and putting them in gelatin caps to get them down painlessly. I don't know what the cop thought as he opened the vast trunk to Mitch's car, which was stuffed with thousands of empty caps contained within a deflated inflatable life raft. After an hour of telling various cops I didn't know any kingpins of the dope world to set up for them on King's Highway in Brooklyn, they turned us loose after confiscating our nickel bag.

I had just reached the car and scooped my joint (our one remaining) up off the street from under the car when the cop came back again. "Oh, shit," I thought. "Changed his mind." He leaned into the window and said in a gruff cop voice, "Have you got any papers?" I gave him my pack of Bambu which he confiscated with a big grin, and was actually rolling a joint as he strolled back to join his fellow fuzz.

Dementia
Bob Wieder

In 1969 I was in a political satire performing group truly worthy of amnesia, called Dementia, and one night after a gig in San Francisco we were heading home in Berkeley on Telegraph Avenue and got pulled over by two Berkeley cops for God knows what in front of the Forum Cafe, whose backyard was People's Park.

They kept asking us what we were up to, and where we'd been, and I'd had a few beers at the gig and had to piss terribly, and finally asked them to let me pop around back of the cafe (it was the wee hours) and take a pee. One cop said okay but he had to pat me down first.

In my shirt pocket he found a matchbox with a lump of hash in it, that being my drug of inspiration at the time. He asked me where I got it, I said some fan had slipped it to me at the gig, I didn't know anything about it, blah blah lie.

He said okay, go pee and come back. I ducked around back, peed and, God knows just why, I came back. When I reappeared around the corner, both cops gaped at me in shock. My return was clearly quite unexpected. They didn't seem to know what to do.

After a brief consultation, they said something like, "Well, it's late, so we'll let you go this time. But we'll just keep this." Meaning the hash, of course, which they did. I suspect they were trolling for stash, and once they'd landed mine, hey, this shift's over. The last thing they wanted was an actual bust to complicate their evening.

Rare Moment

I returned home after my freshman year of college to a small town in Westchester County, New York, with no job, no money, and a girlfriend in tow. Under the circumstances, I was prepared to take whatever job I could find for the summer, and eventually ended up as a maintenance worker at the local dump. I will spare you the details, since you might have eaten recently, but suffice to say that if this is not the worst way to make a minimum wage, it is definitely in the bottom five.

One result of this situation was that I spent a great deal of my time fighting depression by smoking considerable quantities of marijuana, along with several of my friends who were in similarly difficult circumstances. Much of our commiserating took place at Nick's house, as he lived in his own apartment downstairs from his father, and thus enjoyed more freedom of action than the rest of us.

So there we would sit, miserable and stoned, but at least in company, for many hours at a time. Nick had an excellent music collection, and the quality of the dope was very good, as I had maintained my college connections and was supplying the local scene, such as it was. Excitement was rare, to say the least.

This particular evening, I had just picked up an ounce or two of lush green buds, and had brought them to Nick's for a test drive. Now, Nick lived seven miles from anywhere, in the woods on top of a mountain. It wasn't exactly isolated, but I will point out that I once spent the better part of an hour (under the influence of some designer drug) lying in the center of the road outside the house, howling at the moon, and was not disturbed. So we were not expecting visitors as we shared the bong around and listened to early Pink Floyd that night.

At once, Nick announces, "I thought I heard something," and leaves the room. Returning from the entrance hall a moment later, he pokes his head into the cloud of smoke with a look of pure terror on his face and says, "Dave, there's an officer here to see you."

I am holding the steaming bong at the moment he says this. I am very high. I do not immediately understand what he is saying to me, but my girlfriend Karin does, and begins to hide bags of dope under pillows and sofa cushions with remarkable efficiency. At some point she removes the bong from my hand, and I stumble out of the room and into the presence of two Westchester County police officers, who are standing just outside the front door and shining flashlights around the perimeter of the house. I have decided that they are here to tell me that someone in my family has died after being hit by a bus, and am wondering who it is. Or they are here to arrest me, having tracked my drug deal from Manhattan to this house. I brace for the impact of the announcement.

"Is that your car parked out there on the street?" says the lead cop, who is shorter than me and wears a bushy mustache.

"Yes," I reply, curious about what this has to do with my tragically departed family member or impending bust.

"Well, you are parked illegally. I could give you a citation, but instead I'll just ask you to move the car so that..."

I do not hear what he says next, as wave after wave of relief rolls over me. No one is dead, and I am not in any real trouble. His voice continues, and the effect soothes me further. I am nodding gratefully, promising to move the car directly, when suddenly his voice stops. He stiffens, and reaches toward me. I look down at where he is reaching, and notice a bag of dope sticking out of my left breast pocket.

I have just enough time to think, "Oh, shit," which I understand are the most commonly used last words, before his hand reaches my pocket. This is it, I'm going to prison at 19.

He grabs the bag, pushes it down into my pocket, and says, "Put that away where I can't see it."

It is not clear what I did in response to this, although I do recall feeling like my legs were about to buckle. Most likely, I simply grinned like a fool as an enormous love for Westchester County police officers welled up in my breast. I wanted to bow before these men. Had I a son, I would have wished him to become one of them. I'm sure that I once again promised, with great sincerity, to move my car to a proper and highly legal parking space. And after they left, I'm sure I did.

Chapter 20

Almost Busted

Romantic Interlude
Wavy Gravy

It all began lifetimes ago at the Living Theater in New York when I was doing The Phantom Cabaret every Saturday at midnight with Tiny Tim and Moondog.

One night Tiny Tim comes off the stage after 50 minutes of Rudy Vallee, and he says, "Mr. Vallee came inside and he wouldn't leave—I've lost my Crosby power."

And Moondog says, "When I went blind, it was like suffocating."

And, oh, my head is pounding, and I wander outside after the show, and I got this big headache, and there's a burning mattress and a dead cat and broken glass and a guy screaming, "I'm an American, and I killed forty-three Japanese in Iwo Jima," and I stagger into The Fat Black Pussycat, looking for an aspirin, anything.

There's a table of folks sitting around, and they had a big bottle of Excedrin in the middle of the table, and I kicked back six without water to keep my innards crisp. Well, they turned out to be bennies, Benzedrine.

So, three days later, I tried to sneak home before my tongue woke up, and I get in the alley, and this woman says, "Do you wanna get high?"

And I says, "Sure."

She whipped out one of these skinny little cigarettes you didn't see advertised in any magazine, and I lit it up, and we started passing this joint back and forth, and suddenly I'm on the other end of an Ever-Ready flashlight—gotta be the Man behind the light, do not pass Go, do not collect $200—so I swallow the roach and start kissing this strange chick.

Now, I got this roach burning in the back of my tongue, and I got no spit—the bennies have stolen all my spit—so what I have to do is reach my tongue into this strange girl's mouth and scoop out some of her spit to extinguish the roach, which I finally do as the cop says, "All right, you lovers, let's break it up."

State Line
Waldo Steve and the Waldos

A couple of the Waldos were driving from San Francisco to Lake Tahoe in 1972 for some summer fun. The glove box of my 1966 four-door Impala contained a fresh new lid of grass, and in the trunk our suitcases stored two additional lids. As I drove, I expressed my fears about being busted.

One of the Waldos in our car was the son of a cop. In fact, his father was a narcotics officer. Familiar with many of the details of his father's profession, he tried to calm me down by educating me on search-and-seizure laws. We drove for hours, memorizing every detail of California law on search and seizure. I became an expert. Effective knowledge and strategies; nobody was going to bust us. Above all, I remembered that a police officer could not make you open a locked glove box.

We arrived at Lake Tahoe and pulled into the parking lot. The other Waldos got out and went across the street to look for a bathroom. I moved to the passenger side of the front seat and began rolling joints on the lowered glove box lid. All of a sudden, a car door slammed behind me. A cop had pulled in behind and was walking toward the car. I moved fast, rolling up the bag of weed into the box, closing the glove box lid, inserting the key and locking it. I breathed a huge sigh of relief; safe, armed with my new knowledge of search-and-seizure laws.

The officer knocked on the window. I rolled it down and he asked for license and registration. I complied. He returned them and asked, "What's in the glove box?"

"Maps," I answered.

The cop said, "Let me see those maps."

"No," I said.

He said, "Open up the glove box."

"I don't have to," I said.

He said, "Yes you do."

I said, "California law number 66294 (or whatever the number was at the time) says that I do not have to open a locked glove box."

And he said, "You're in Nevada, boy!"

I looked over my right shoulder. The state line was about 20 yards away. I looked over my other shoulder to see that two more cop cars had arrived, including an unmarked narc car. I opened the glove box and handed over the lid. The officer handed the lid to the cop from the unmarked car who started examining it closely.

The narc remarked, "Doesn't look too good. Too many seeds and stems."

One of the cops then said to me, "I'm going to give you a choice. If you have any more weed in this automobile, you can hand it all over to us right now and we may or we may not bust you. Or, we can search your car and if we should find anything we will definitely bust you." He added, "It's your Nevada gamble."

I opened up the trunk and handed over the two lids.

The narc officer asked me, "Do you want a receipt for this?"

And I responded, "Do you give trading stamps too?"

He chuckled.

The three officers had a little meeting while I waited patiently. Then one of them walked over and showed me a children's school-style notebook with a list of names and numbers written in it. He started writing my name at the bottom of the list.

He said, "I'm going to give you exactly one minute to get across that border. You are number 324 in the state of Nevada and you cannot come back to Nevada for as long as you live."

I said, "What about my friends? How will they find me?"

Holding up his watch, he said, "You have one minute to get out of Nevada, starting now."

I raced to the state line border marker located on the sidewalk next to the casinos at Lake Tahoe's South Shore and waited. About a half hour later my friends walked up.

We really wanted to go to Nevada because Nevada had the best beaches. We spent the entire following day trying to find a lawyer. Nearly every attorney we contacted would not talk to us. A few said they would talk with us; however, they quoted astronomical rates we could not afford. We were frustrated, but determined to get an answer as to whether or not I could enter Nevada for the rest of eternity.

The next day we drove over to the North Shore of Tahoe. An attorney there agreed to talk to us for a reasonable price. We were excited because this one attorney who agreed to see us was named Joseph Joynt. We paid our money up front, and waited on pins and needles to ask him, "Could we go back into Nevada?"

He answered with one word: "Probably."

We drove directly to Nevada and spent the rest of our vacation there, knowing the entire time what it feels like to be an outlaw.

The Favor
St. Gerard

Fred and I had struck out again on a Friday night, and we were leaving the bar. It was snowing lightly as we were walking to the car. As we passed two attractive females, I said, "Typical, we are walking out and two pretties are walking in." They chuckled and we struck up a nice conversation.

A few minutes later, the four of us were in Fred's snow-covered car, rolling a fatty. Suddenly there was a flashlight banging on the window, knocking the snow off. A state trooper was ordering the four of us out of the car.

As he was getting ready to bust us on a minor possession charge, a car flew into the parking lot with a long-haired guy screaming, "Officers, there is a car hanging over the bridge up the street, there are people in it, and it looks like it's going to fall into the river!"

The cops looked at each other, then at us, and then one said, "Look, get out of here, stay out of here, and never let me see this car around here again." With that, he put the pot in his pocket and sped off toward the bridge.

The long-hair looked at us and said, "You owe me one. Get out of here before he finds out I was fucking with him. If you ever see me on the side of the road, do me a return favor." With that he was gone.

I looked at the two ladies and said, "Where should we go from here?" The one's reply was, "Straight to Hell, asshole." It was another typical Friday night for Fred and me.

Chapter 21

Busted

Fish Cops

We had planned a heavy recreational schedule that day which included hiking, dinner out and a Neil Young concert. It was the early 1980s, and money, not pleasure, was beginning to rule people's lives. That hadn't caught on with us yet, so we had rolled three or four joints to enhance our enjoyment of the day's activities.

We decided to stop by an out-of-the-way place we'd visited for just such an occasion many times before. It was a non-developed area outside the sprawling city; no homes, businesses or schools anywhere around. It was almost a mile-long walk on the unmarked trail from a county road to a quiet, wooded spot on the lake shore. There was no one nearby, just some boats way out on the lake.

While we were indulging, I recalled a conversation I'd had with a coworker about law enforcement personnel, specifically Conservation Officers, whom we referred to derogatorily as "Fish Cops." My coworker told me that C.O.'s had more law enforcement authority than any other group: sheriffs, state police, city police— that is, they could arrest you at any time for anything. I was young and naive in those days, and mistakenly assumed the scope of their authority was hunting and fishing violations. This was news to me, and I was relaying the information to my companion while we smoked.

Before we finished inhaling, there was a noise in the woods behind us, and who should appear but two Conservation Officers, who promptly confiscated our small supply of medicinal herbs and arrested us for possession of marijuana. Bummer. While they were conducting the honors, one said, "So, just talking about us, huh?" Like Big Brother, they had been lurking nearby in the woods, listening to us the entire time. Serious bummer.

Who knows what they were doing there? Looking for people fishing without a license, couples "doing it," or maybe dopers like us. We'd never encountered anyone else in the area during previous visits. It was a long, silent, humiliating walk back to the car with our new friends trailing behind us. Miraculously, they didn't search the car, which didn't matter since it was clean anyway. No doubt the story still circulates amongst drunken C.O.'s at cop parties even to this day. It's easy to collar people who aren't going to fight back.

So, the major losses were: all shreds of dignity; three joints; a nice roach clip; a good high and buoyant mood; and the $500 each we paid our lawyer to intervene on our behalf while appearing later before the local judge. He obtained for us one year of good-behavior probation, and no conviction. And so we managed to be good and made sufficient reparation for the serious harm we inflicted upon society, that being appreciating the gifts of the Earth by sharing a joint in the woods, off the beaten path, bothering no one.

Surprisingly, we have not become deranged dope fiends as depicted in *Reefer Madness*, but remain "productive members of society," for what it's worth.

Most Likely to Succeed

Eleven nice plants in the ground. August, the late 1980s—5:30 a.m.—Mendocino, California. The COMMET squad bursts into my house, waking me up from a sleep that still has four hours to go. They hold me at gunpoint as I pull on my trousers.

A couple of their guys yell back to the house from the garden and confirm what the aerial photos had given them reason to suspect: this person is, indeed, a cultivator of marijuana.

As I listen to the swipes of their machetes putting an end to my short career as a dope farmer, I am told to sit at my dining-room table and keep my hands where they can see them. They ask me to produce some identification.

On the table in front of me is my high school yearbook, which I had been thumbing through the night before in anticipation of attending my 25th reunion a month later. I slide the book over and open it to the page that shows me in my blue and gold FFA jacket posing with the girl who, like me, had been voted "Most Likely to Succeed."

"There," I said, pointing to the picture. "That's me."

I think the deputy in charge of the bust cracked a tiny smile as she glanced at the photograph, but it was gone an instant later.

I was sentenced to 90 days. I did 47 of them and was released for good behavior and because the jail was overcrowded, largely because of arrests and convictions of other small growers and traffickers.

The part that hurts the most is that today, more than 10 years later, in a community I have served in many positive ways—as an artist, an educator, a worker for worthy causes—people still have a tendency to think of me first as "that guy who did some time for growing back in the '80s." And, sadly, no matter what I may do or accomplish in the years to come, that simple fact will probably never change.

A Tale of Two Busts

In 1962, I was sitting in the lotus position in front of a large mirror trying to disappear, and Robin says, "Chic, someone's banging on my bedroom wall, and something is coming through the wall." I got up and went to the far wall of her room where there was a hole six inches in diameter that now had a bulging plastic bag beginning to protrude. I heard my neighbor yell, "Hey, man, hold on to this till the cops leave. They're coming in my front door!"

Meanwhile, Robin says, "Someone's banging on our door!" I quickly took three dime bags of my personal herb stash, tossed them out the window to recover later, and answered the door. It was a policeman who said, "Are these apartments connected?" I said, "No," but he wanted to check anyway. He came into the kitchen and said, "What's that noise in there?"

"I don't know."

Then he looks at the hole in the wall, sees the bag protruding and then break, and a hand comes through trying to cram the rest. The cop says, "What is it?"

"I don't know."

"Pick it up!"

"Oh, no," I say. "You pick it up. It's all yours. I don't even know what it is."

The cop grabbed the biggest bunch of it and disappeared back out to the storefront.

Robin said, "There's still about two ounces on the floor. What are you going to do?"

"No choice. I have to go out there and watch the bust go down and act surprised."

I walked down the tile hall, through the large wood and glass door, down the corrugated iron steps, where I stood by the banister, propped up by a couple of my Puerto Rican brothers who knew what was going down.

After the cops took away fellow members of the Living Theater cast of The Brig and a couple of my other friends, I went back inside and wondered what to do about the grass remaining on the floor of Robin's bedroom. Little by little, we smoked it all. The cops never came back.

When I discovered that my three dime bags were not where I tossed them, I went out into the street and found one of my hermanos, Kimo, and asked him to put out the word that they were my bags. A half hour later, my friend Victor shows up with two $15 bags and says, "I'm sorry, Chico, I didn't know it was your stash. We thought it was ditched from the bust."

I said, "No hay problema, amigo," and gave him one of the

bags. I loved my life on the Lower East Side. I loved our *barrio*. Good people.

Hash Police

In 1967 I was living in Hell's Kitchen. As an aspiring actor, I was compelled to sell grass, hash and acid to augment my lifestyle. One day, three plainclothes police came to my door with a search warrant, seized my stash, and took me and a friend to the local precinct lock-up for later transport to the Tombs.

After my initial interrogation, they knew I would tell them nothing they could use. They were angry, but they knew I wasn't a rat. The two older cops—one Irish, one Italian—left the room first, followed by the young Italian and myself. The young cop gestured with his eyes to the table in the room as we were leaving and said, "I didn't see anything."

I looked and saw a small piece of my hash just sitting there. I figured what the hell and picked it up and mashed it into the right hinge of my glasses and went to the holding cell to wait. I told my friend what happened and we were puzzled together.

Then the young cop walked by our cell and squeezed a horizontal bar and walked away snickering. He had stuck another piece of hash to the bars. I quickly molded my other hinge.

Later, when they took us to the Tombs, they gave us our own private cell away from the junkies and assholes, and we spent the whole night smoking little pieces of hash on a straight pin. I even managed to smuggle in a pen and wrote a song lyric on a piece of hanger cardboard.

Corrupting Minors
Maximum Traffic

I got a job and my first apartment when I was 18 years old. Only weeks after moving into the place, the local cops came and forced in my door, knocking me on my butt. They tore the place apart, throwing all my clothes on the floor, overturning my bed. They looked in every nook and cranny. When they were done, they asked me if I wanted them to get a search warrant.

They found a full ounce of weed in my pocket and another ounce floating in the toilet. I had some friends visiting, and one of them—my best friend, Ray, who was only 16 years old—had the presence of mind to try to flush one of the bags. Unfortunately, he emptied the bag into the toilet and flushed, but the damn thing never did flush very efficiently, and the weed was just swirling around and around.

One burly cop burst into the bathroom and yelled, "That's evidence! You fish that out of there!"

To my astonishment, my buddy Ray yelled right back, "If you want it so bad, you fish it out of there!"

Scared as I was, I had to fight back the laughter. They decided to leave the evidence.

The cops took us all to the city jail where they questioned us late into the night, trying to get us to rat on our friends. While sitting in the front office of the police station, Ray started to freak out. Even though he was only 16, he was a stocky kid, heavier than me. He never even touched any kind of dope, but his adrenaline suddenly kicked in.

He got up from the seat and started growling in a very menacing way. He walked over to the counter and started pounding on it. Instantly the room was filled with cops. Ray was bellowing like a mad bull, and he was throwing the cops around like popcorn! It took a three-cop pile-up to subdue and handcuff him. All the while the cops are screaming, "What kind of dope is he on?" No dope at all.

Well, when the dust settled, I was charged with corrupting minors because I was the only one who was 18 and legally an adult. They later dropped the charges down to possession. I got thrown out of the apartment, lost my job, and got a year's probation and a $50 fine.

I was outraged. I knew that the revolution was here and that this kind of bullshit oppression was soon to be a thing of the past. Just goes to show you how wrong a person can be.

Chapter 22

Serving Time

Escaping Reality
Dennis Sobin

Fortunately, when I was asked to make a contribution to this book, I was in an ideal place to get others more experienced than myself to write. Being in prison, I knew a lot of guys who had done lots of dope, both before and during their prison stay.

I wasted little time circulating the letter I had received asking for pot stories. Then a funny thing happened at the prison. The shit hit the fan, quite coincidentally. The factory here that makes license plates for the state of Florida motor vehicle bureau got busted.

It seems that the inmates who worked there had a terrific scam going. They stole plates to ship to criminal contacts on the outside, people who would sell them to practicing libertarians who preferred not to register their cars with a government agency.

The payment these inmates received for their handiwork was pot. Everything was handled through the shipping and receiving department of the prison factory, staffed by clever inmates. Who knows what went wrong?

At any rate, the scheme got exposed about the time I started passing around the letter. As a result, paranoia ran high and a major source of pot stories closed up. Too bad, too. Prison is about the safest place to do dope since it's practically impossible to infiltrate by undercover cops.

The real trick is to get it in, but as long as people seek to escape reality—as they most surely do here—that will happen. Just the fact of using dope in prison seems pretty funny to me.

Lipton
Frederic Berthoff

I'm writing from the federal prison here in Miami, five years into a
21-year sentence for hashish and marijuana trafficking. You hear a
lot about drugs in jail, but at these new places security is pretty
tight, so there's not much around. I'd smell pot at night once in a
while but it was rare. So, when offered a joint for free, I should
have known it was a gaff.

Jose lived upstairs on the corner and was a cheerful little Puerto
Rican who spoke English like he was born here. He was in charge
of the only set of colored pencils on the block so I knew him a little
bit through that avenue. I used to borrow them sometimes and
give him cigarettes for the favor.

Like most of the wheeler-dealers on the block, Jose mixed it up
pretty good and still had a black eye that had been healing for a
couple of weeks. I had the colored pencils from the night before
and was bringing them back to his room before we went out to
recreation in the morning. In his cell he pulled a wispy-thin jay-bar
(joint) out from behind a protruding ear and gave a conspiratorial
leer.

They say nothing's for nothing, especially in the can, but I liked
the kid so I figured, "All right, gimme the fucking thing," and took
it. I brought a cigar and a lighter outside with me, looking forward
to a good smoke despite the paranoia that I was way too old to
enjoy any more.

Outside we had a choice of four cages to spend the hour in. The
crowd from the cellblock divvied up mostly along age and color
lines, but there was nothing formal or set about it. Each cage was
a half-court with a hoop, and that day I went over to the farthest
one where Jose and the young kids of darker hues played.

So I lit up my El Producto and took a few puffs, taking a quick
look around for the screws. Then out came the joint, looking
pathetically small compared to the cigar, and I lit it too. I took a
couple of deep drags and let the sweet smoke out my nose like I
always did to taste the quality. Old habits are hard to break.

I savored it like a wine steward wearing his little silver cup on a
chain. It was sweet and kind of green tasting, but too dry for
green pot, and yet it tasted familiar, like something from a long
time ago. Smoke curled into the air and rolled indiscreetly downwind. Familiar, familiar.

I had a bamboo opium pipe that my mom bought in the Village
back in the '40s for a souvenir. She'd given it to me when I was a
teenybopper and over the years I had smoked a little of everything
in it, though it had never been degraded with "the rock." Banana

peels, oregano, for starters, then later, several varieties of pot and hash, some opium (once, I think), psilocybin mushrooms, Sir Walter Raleigh Kentucky Burley, and one time, tea.

I was listening to a Simon and Garfunkel song about how they "smoke a pint of tea a day," and I knew they were talking about weed, but on a boring afternoon I threw a pinch of Earl Grey into the little brass bowl and fired it up. A long, long time ago, but that day in the cage there it was again. The taste of tea.

Bobby was a young black wiseguy who'd just been booted out of Pilgrim County Jail for fighting and sent up to Littleton. He wore his hair in little twists on top of his head with the sides shaved, as was the style. We were talking about the past week when I was playing hoop barefoot and he was laughing at me with his buddies. "Yo, look at this dude...." So he knew me and when he smelled the joint he came hopping over, flashing his trademark troublemaker's grin.

"Hey, man, I smell that shit, Man. Where'd you get that?"

It wouldn't have been cool to say just where, so I didn't and shrugged it off.

"Somebody gave it to me."

"You pay for it?" He was laughing now just like he did at the dude playing barefoot. "Never mind, I knows where you got it, man. Hey, yo, Lipton!" He was calling to my main man, my connection, Jose. "Hey, yo, Lipton!"

Jose came over from the game, knowing he was bagged (in trouble) and already looking at his shoes.

"Hey, yo, man, you still passin' that shit? You passin' that shit off on my man here?"

Jose—"Lipton"—looked so bad that I stuck up for him even though the jig was up.

I said, "Well, Bobby, he gave it to me for nothing."

"That motherfucker passin' that shit out for weed, why you think he got a black eye? Motherfuckers caught him passin' that tea last week for money and fucked him up."

Jose skulked back to the game and Bobby was hollering after him, "Hey, yo, Lipton!...Lipton!"

It reminded me of the Eskimos I'd learned about in school. My anthropology teacher was a hands-on guy and he went up to Alaska for an extended tour of field research with a primitive tribe up there. When one of the Eskimos got out of line they punished him by assigning a derogatory name, related to the offense, for a specified period of time. A guy caught stealing someone else's kayak was called "Stealer of Kayak" for a full year.

So I guess these kids in prison had unknowingly adopted a universal code of behavior modification for their own use. They added a beating, which the Eskimos chose not to. Call that the barbarian influence.

Anyway, Lipton still had the pencils, and the gaff joint was for free, so after a couple of days of ball-breaking I went back to calling him Jose. Bobby didn't let me forget so easily. He'd see me coming and say, "Hey, yo, man, you smokin' any good reefer lately? Where's your boy, Lipton? Ha ha ha!"

Chapter 23

Miscellaneous Joints

Good Vibes
Stephen Gaskin

One of the neatest hippie communes I ever lived in was a house in Stinson Beach on Highway 1 just north of San Francisco. It was a nice two-story house in a little ravine that went up Mt. Tam behind the house. Off the left of the house there was a grove of pine trees that was host to a herd of Monarch butterflies. On the other side of the house there was a river of Nasturtiums whose flowers were the same colors as the butterflies.

It was a lovely hippie house and had three couples and a few singles of hippies and hippie wannabes living there. Paul and Pamela were an art student and a yogi. Charlie and Linda were the resident non-vegetarians. Linda had a liver condition and was under doctor's orders to eat meat. Charlie was much too loyal to let Linda be the only non-veggie. And there was Margaret and me.

I say wannabes because we would have done a better job of having some grass around if we were more serious hippies. We had been out for a while. One of the single men wasn't doing well at all without grass. He bitched and moaned and whined until we all said, "If you aren't going to do anything about it, just shut up."

Joe, the single man, admitted that he had some money and said, "Well, if none of you guys have enough gumption to do something about it, I will." And he took off for the city to buy a kilo of Acapulco Gold, which cost $250.

While Joe was gone, Linda told me that I didn't really understand about her rat. I thought I did. I mean a rat is a rat. That was actually the attitude she was complaining about. She took me into the kitchen and got her rat out of the cage on top of the fridge.

"Look," she said, "notice his tail. There is not a scale or hair out of place. Look at his feet and claws, just perfect!"

As she showed me her rat, I saw that she was right. The rat was beautiful, intelligent, friendly, clean and sweet-smelling. He was an excellent rat. Linda and I got on well after I understood her rat.

That evening we saw the car Joe had taken to town coming up the drive. When Joe left the car, he had such a jaunty air and such a good vibe that we caught eyes with each other and lifted eyebrows. It must be really good stuff, we thought.

Joe came into the house.

"Well," we said, "where is it?"

"Where is what?" he said.

"The pot!" we said.

"Oh, that. Well, I didn't actually get any."

We were confused. His good vibes seemed to persist.

"What happened?" we demanded.

"I got robbed."

We freaked out. "Wow, man, what a drag." We were mystified. His good vibes remained evident.

Joe said, "I met these guys and asked about dope and they took me in this alley and robbed me."

He continued to smile. We had to ask, "What the hell are you smiling about?"

"They didn't hurt me!"

Joe's good vibes and attitude adjustment lasted so long that we decided that he had gotten his money's worth out of his dope adventure. He might not have been so sweet for so long if he had actually scored.

Ms. Deal
Dawna Kaufmann

I've learned, as a comedy writer in Hollywood, if ya wanna be a player, it helps to be a player, which is why my writer pal Jason's weekly poker game has for years been great for off-duty shmoozing with the TV elite. His regular group consists of an Agent, a Director, a Producer and a Star, with an occasional drop-in. Whenever I'd try to wheedle an invitation, Jason would snipe that they "don't play with girls," which would cue my lecture on affirmative action.

After hearing this argument a zillion times, Jason finally relented and agreed to let me attend that coming Thursday's session, if, as he said, I could "cut it." Ha! Cut it? I can cut it, shuffle it and deal it, I chortled, as I promised to show up at 7:30 p.m. And bring cash 'cause they "don't take checks or credit cards"—as if I was gonna lose!

During the week I bought a poker book, memorizing important things like the author's name, Scarne, which rhymes with Carney, and rules and strategy for the game. It reinforced my feeling that you can't fear high stakes—it's all relative, and winning is proportional to skill. Play your odds. Bet intelligently. Know when to fold 'em, know when to hold 'em. I felt "in the chips" already, but bought a Kenny Rogers CD for extra inspiration.

It wasn't like I hadn't played before—I'd racked up hundreds of hours on my Video Poker for Windows program—I just hadn't played with humans. As long as I had my little card that says what beats what, and can keep straight which way is clockwise, I could reasonably take on these manly men. Besides, I've always been convinced of female supremacy, a point on which no male's ever agreed with me, and on behalf of sisterhood everywhere, I welcomed the challenge of pitting my shrewd intellect against their macho egoism. Prepare to die, scoundrels!

So, it's Thursday night and Jason introduces me to the crew. I come on strong, singing, from *Guys and Dolls*, "Where's the action, where's the game? Gotta have the game or we'll die from shame," but when they don't react, I figure they're not theater people. As we take our places around the table, the Director wisely suggests I watch the action a bit first. Right away I'm impressed with the speed of things. In the time it takes them to rotate around the table so that each player gets to select a dealer's choice game, I'd still be dealing one hand. Whew!

The Producer mentions white chips are $1, reds $5 and blues $10, and while I rationally accept that, emotionally all I see is a patriotic pile of rent money in the middle of the table. The Star hands me a beer in a can, and I'm glad he doesn't patronize me by asking if I want a glass like some sissy, although actually I would've liked one—so sue me. Despite their banter, there's a thickness in the air. I resist suggesting we turn on the nearby TV for *Friends*, fearing they might throw it, and me, out the window. Concentrate, concentrate, I beg myself.

You know that feeling you get when your instinct for survival is threatened and you're forced to rely on devious and drastic weapons to stay alive? Well, it occurs to me that I have in my purse one of the fattest joints in captivity, and not only is it a bomber, it's Maui Wowie. Certain that I'll have these clowns on their knees in moments, I light up, inhale deeply and pass the joint to the guys. "No thanks," they mutter and echo. They don't smoke dope?—I'm screwed!

Not to seem a fool by putting it out now, I keep toking, each hit of the potent gold forming a cosmic key that unlocks corridors of mutinous brain cells which are, at this very moment, lining up single file and jumping like kamikaze parachutists out of my eyes and ears and into the poker chip quicksand. Whereas I originally couldn't wait to get into the game, my head's now so clogged I suspect someone's poured bacon grease in my ears.

An hour later, I know they're wondering when I'll join the game, a thought which crosses my mind too. They play on, perfectly aware of the impact of each newly dealt card, knowing exactly which raise they're on and how every hand's financial history is recorded—as I sit there, blitzed, pressing my body hard into the plastic of the kitchen chair, hoping that instead of me, they'll see just another orange daisy on the pattern.

How I wish I could astrally project myself home. What a perfect opportunity this would be to clean my oven; I'd been meaning to disengage that exploded baked potato residue from 1995. My enfeebled brain drifts back to their game, still vicious as ever. I'm not sure if it's a mean ruse to bilk me out of my humble life savings, but the Agent speaks up to see if I'm ready to play. My senses prepare for Red Alert but my mouth settles for Automatic Pilot and I meekly mumble, "Any minute now..." Nuts! Here's my chance to score points for feminism and I'm blowing it. What would Gloria Steinem do if she were here? And would she play with Queens higher than Kings? While contemplating this, I sense Jason's displeasure that I'm not in the game. After all, he promised these gung-ho gamblers a fellow Amarillo Slim, not some gutless lookie-loo with the canny aptitude of a blow-up doll. Plus Jason's losing—Lady Luck, I'm not. I try to steady my gaze and study their game, but it's no use. With cards flying at warp speed and chips clicking like a St. Vitus flamenco dancer, my already pathetic attention span's in urgent need of new elastic.

Just then—miracles of miracles—my cell phone rings. I answer it:
It's a wrong number, but I don't tell the fellas. "Hi," I lie into the
receiver. "Oh, no! I'll be there in ten minutes!" With a whimper I
announce that my father's in the hospital and I must go to him.
They all understand—especially Jason, who attended my dad's
funeral several years ago but mercifully keeps my secret.

As I head to the door I state boldly, "Gentlemen," then weaken
like a fist without bones. "I...I really planned to take all your
money tonight, but, uh, now that I've watched you, I gotta admit
I'm nowhere near your league. Unless you're willing to play open-
handed till I catch up [like in 2012]—it's better for me to just cut
my losses and thank you for a most educational evening." My
embarrassment is cut short by a genuine release of tension, with
laughter and good cheer replacing the formerly serious facades.
They chatter about how much ahead they'd be if they were only
smart like me, and Jason winks that he wants to borrow my cell
phone. I make my escape, never mentioning the script I'd planned
to pitch them, and head home to destroy my collection of Vegas
junket brochures and immediate plans for world domination.

It there's a moral to this story—and I'm not sure there is—it's
that poker and pot don't mix. At least for me, at least that night.
But I'm happy to say Video Poker for Windows and pot mix just
dandy, and that's what I did when I got home, and have done fre-
quently since. There are just some pleasures one should not live
without.

Smoking Pot in the White House
Steve Diamond

Certain cities have a mystical aura, such as New York, Paris, Rome, Rio, Tokyo and Washington, to name a few. In DC, tourists stop and pose their families before the big iron fence in front of the White House and snap away. This phenomenon allows these visitors to take a little magic home and put it on their mantle.

It was 1977, and an early spring made DC a city of flowers. The traditional cherry blossoms, azaleas, tulips and lilacs flowered in profusion, giving Washington the smell of an arboretum. I was working as executive director and lobbyist for a nationwide association of doctors headquartered in Washington, DC.

The Carter administration was a group of likeable boobs. President Carter fanatically believed that if something was right, in a Biblical way, it would grow like mushrooms and become law. While this simple optimism worked in church, it would never do the job in Congress. Deals were made—"I'm for you, you're for me." Carter's lobbyists in the Congress believed the same scripture.

Carter won in 1976 because he was considered an outsider. Gerald Ford, of course, spent over 30 years in the House of Representatives. Carter won because Ford pardoned Nixon. Ford was attempting to put the government, shaken by Nixon's fascist regime, back to normal. Ford was attempting to heal the war wounds of Watergate.

My Uncle Bunny, a veteran of World War II, was in the 82nd Airborne division—a storied outfit which was on the front lines of the war, from Italy to the Battle of the Bulge and beyond. I remember something he once told me as we listened to a Cubs game on the radio.

"Stevie," he laughed and lamented, "near the end of World War II, we marched through Germany. As the inhabitants begged for cigarettes and chocolate, they all would say, 'Hitler was a bad man and I'm not a party member and I fought to overthrow him.' There wasn't a Nazi civilian in sight."

Similarly, in the mid-'70s, nobody in Washington had been a Nixon backer or even a Republican. They had no idea what Tricky Dick was doing in that consecrated White House to destroy our democracy.

Through my work, I often met for dinner with Don Harvey, Carter's health advisor. He was from South Carolina, had a country drawl and wore Brooks Brothers suits. His prize possession was a roofless Corvair—the car Ralph Nader called a moving death trap.

Harvey invited me to do dinner in his closet-sized office at the White House and tour the premises because only a few staffers worked past 10. He was the tour leader, and we saw the offices of

Dr. Peter Bourne (he had been dismissed because he proffered a prescription for Quaaludes to a pretty, young secretary), Zbignew Brezinsky, Burt Lance and the whole sorry crew.

Unfortunately for his inexperienced administration, Carter and his Major Domo, Hamilton Jordan, made the tough decisions. Carter hired many of his cronies from Georgia to fill policy-vetted sensitive positions.

Don's office was on the lower level of the building. It sported English windows three-quarters of the way up the wall and had no view, except of the Secret Service guards. Don and I walked up to the Rose Garden, planted by Jackie Onassis, which was so small it made me sad.

Remember, this was pre-crack, and many of the '60s activists expected marijuana prohibition to end soon. Half the people in the country found it mildly relaxing and an appetite enhancer. They laughed at the movie *Reefer Madness* made by Harry Anslinger and adopted by J. Edgar Hoover, the director of the FBI who denied that the Mafia ever existed.

Harvey made a small joke about this house being the safest place in America. He reached into the inside pocket of his made-to-measure suit and pulled out a huge reefer.

"You like the weed, don't you, Stevie?"

"Sure," I said, "but not here in the White House surrounded by cops, Secret Service and executive-protection gumshoes."

Harvey asked, "Do you have a match?"

"No, but I've got a Bic lighter in my trenchcoat. You can keep it. Bob, I'm going home—thanks, but no thanks."

"Steve, you're a rookie in this town. Look up at the windows." I took off my glasses, which improved my astigmatic eyes, and I saw shoes moving back and forth next to the windows. "Relax, man. Do you see the shoes?"

"Yes, of course."

"Which way are the heels pointing?"

"Outward," I whispered.

"Steve, their job isn't to bust us. They never involve themselves in our business. They're looking out on that crowd of stalkers that could cause harm to the chief executive."

Scrabbled
Maximum Traffic

Whitey's house was shared by a half-dozen guys, truck drivers and construction workers. They all smoked weed, a lot of weed. There were bags of weed all over the house. Everywhere there was an ashtray, there was a bag of weed. Little bags and big bags. They told me to smoke all I wanted. All these guys were a few years older than me, and most of them a hundred pounds heavier, and I was kind of nervous. They drank a whole lot of beer and smoked a whole lot of pot, and I got even more nervous.

There was a wired-up Mexican guy there who started hounding everyone to play Scrabble with him. They all just kept laughing at him and telling him that he couldn't spell in English anyway. He started getting really mad, so to cool him off, his buddies told him that I would play Scrabble with him. I could hardly refuse; actually I was afraid to refuse.

So I sat down at the kitchen table with this bad-tempered, wound-up, drunk Mexican construction worker and set up the Scrabble game. I had taken two years of Spanish in high school so I asked the guy if he would like to play using Spanish words. He instantly became friendly to me. "Hermano! You know Español!"

He fired up another joint and started to play. Well, the guy was a terrible Scrabble player and within a dozen plays I was miles ahead of him even though we were playing in Spanish. It turned out that his friendly feelings toward me were very short-lived. He jumped up from his chair and threw the Scrabble board at my head, scattering pieces all over the room. "You mother-lucking cheater," he screamed at me. I ran for my life. His buddies all grabbed him and held him off me, but they were all laughing hysterically. The drunk Mexican didn't like it one bit. That was enough party for me. I told Whitey that I was tired and asked him where I could sleep. He took me to an unused attic room with a nice cot.

I was just starting to calm down when someone knocked on the door. It was a plain-looking girl, maybe 10 years older than me. She walked in and sat on the cot. The guys downstairs had decided that they should provide me with a woman. I was 17 years old and had never had my clothes off around a woman...and I didn't have the nerve to start with a total stranger. She was sweet and tried to talk me into it. A woman trying to talk me into sex—now that was a first.

So, you might imagine, this kind of experience changed my perspective on the world a bit. It made me feel a lot less "white bread and corn-fed." When I came back to my hometown I felt that I belonged to a much bigger community than the one I had left behind. And that community was very fond of smoking dope.

Miracle Cure
Robert DeLancy

I am 42 years old. In 1986, when I was 29, I suffered a stroke. An aneurysm, to be exact. The doctors performed a right frontal lobotomy. The blood vessel they had clipped, the following day, let go. It broke. Needless to say, I suffered another stroke. Much more severe. They gave me less than a 1% chance of even making it to the operating table. They had already told my parents I was not going to make it.

As I am writing this, you can see that I survived. I was a vegetable for a while. It was like being born again. I had to learn to walk, talk, eat, think and see. Just everything. Of all the visitors I'm told I had, I did not know anyone was even there. My sister tells me how I would just lay there looking right through her, as the drool dripped from my mouth.

I was a non-functioning vegetable, until about a week after the operation, when my good buddy, George, stopped in to see me. But first I must tell you, the doctors did say that I would definitely have some stroke effects because of the severity of the stroke. Like a drooped mouth, or the loss of function in one or more limbs.

Anyway, my friend George comes walking in my room. He had no idea what kind of condition I was in. I had no idea that there was even anybody there. Not just yet. A little while later I realized that he had asked me if I wanted a hit off his one-hitter. Somehow I understood, and conveyed a yes. He lifted me up off the bed into my wheelchair, and rolled me over to the window.

I took two hits, back to back. Almost instantly, I snapped back to reality. I then remembered him coming into the room, and what followed. Instantly, I knew who he was, and what he was saying. Instead of just drooling, I started communicating. At least the best that I could.

It was like, at that instant, my brain started functioning. I knew what was going on around me. I was actually thinking. Those two hits were absolutely a miracle for me. Since I have never heard of any other cases like mine, I thought that this might possibly be another area for the medical community to explore.

I truly believe, if not for those two hits, I would be a vegetable. It took me 14 months to fully recover. I never had any stroke effects. At first I was taking Dilanten to prevent seizures. But I still had a couple. When I was released, I was getting high and taking my Dilanten. After about three months, I stopped taking the pills.

I went about a year with no problems. Then a dry spell hit. No weed to be found. On my fifth dry day, I had a seizure. Which was like a truck parking on my head, and my body shook profusely. A friend came through later that evening. And I have been high ever since. And never another seizure. I truly believe this is something that should be looked into. I believe it could possibly benefit other stroke victims.

Speaking of Talking
David McReynolds

As a recovered (or recovering) alcoholic, I know there is one thing marijuana and vodka have in common—you get earthshaking insights when you get high. The huge difference between vodka and marijuana is that in the morning, when you are sober and dealing with the hangover from vodka, the insights are forgotten, buried under a wave of nausea, while even 40 years later I can remember in detail the insights from my first encounter with marijuana.

It was in Ocean Park, California, the little Bohemia by the sea where as a UCLA student I'd taken up residence in one of the cheap shacks (cheap? hell, it didn't even have warm water or a shower). A student friend, Bruce, a poet and a radical who had been expelled from Max Shachtman's Trotskyist Socialist Youth League for being queer, had asked if I wanted to try marijuana. I said sure.

We went to his shack and lit up. There were no hallucinations. I didn't feel light, or think I was floating. But I did realize that as we talked I had the distinct impression that just out of my line of sight, to my right, was a golden wheat field in Kansas, viewed through an open window, while to my left, again just out of the line of sight, was a doorway leading downstairs to Le Club Tabu in Paris, which I'd visited on my first trip to Europe in 1951.

If I actually turned to the right, there was only the wall of Bruce's shack, with an art print tacked to it, and if I turned to the left, there was only another wall. Not a hallucination—just a simple certainty that as I sat in that little room, I had Paris off to one side, and Kansas to the other.

And I became aware that...I couldn't talk. I could see the words in my head drift off, assume shapes, become animals, sheep or cats, and wander into my unconscious. A simple sentence—such as "I find it hard to talk"—couldn't be completed because as soon as I stepped past "I find," the words had begun to drift away, and the next word, "it," refused to appear.

I was stranded on whatever word I had last spoken. I couldn't reach back, and I couldn't reach ahead. I couldn't even say "I have forgotten what I was going to say." I might get as far as "forgotten" and found I didn't know where that sentence had begun, nor where it was headed.

I became keenly aware of the fact that the mind was a time machine, that for a brief period of a few seconds, the past, present and future coexisted absolutely. The only way any of us can talk is because we remember precisely the last words we spoke, and because we know in advance precisely the words we are about to speak.

That which was objective reality only a moment earlier—my voice, which could have been recorded on tape, and which has, the instant I've finished speaking and the sound waves have faded and gone flat, ceased to have any objective reality—remains objective reality inside my brain. And those words which do not yet have objective reality—the words I have not yet spoken—are objectively real inside my brain.

That objective reality doesn't extend far in either direction. While I know what I've just said, with each passing moment the past becomes more variable and, barring a tape recording, memory becomes uncertain. And while I know what I'm about to say—for the next few instants—beyond that, the future also becomes variable.

My sentences may shift and change because of some event—a comment by Bruce, with whom I'm smoking dope, some outside event such as a dog barking, anything which might disrupt the direction in which my conversation had been headed.

However, for the brief period of a few seconds, what I have just said, what I am in the process of saying, and what I'm about to say all coexist in the brain. Which makes the mind, not in some figurative sense, but in a real way, a time machine, in which dimensions which we thought could never meet, coexist.

Whether I've been able to explain this so that it makes sense to you, I don't know. But 40 years later it is as clear to me as it was that night.

There are, of course, other experiences which I'm sure are common—music may make sense in new ways, making love becomes more pleasurable, more deeply involving. What marijuana is not good for is playing poker, where players can become more fascinated by the shapes and colors of their hand than by whether the five cards add up to anything that can win.

When I drank, I found I could play excellent poker up to the point I passed out. In social gatherings, alcohol is a social drug. A glass of wine and you relax, the group becomes more animated, more interactive. With marijuana the group becomes less social, as people drift into private worlds—in the words of Quentin Crisp, "marijuana is a distancer."

Research Project
Robert Altman

"Would you like to collaborate, Robert?"

This query was extended by my seatmate, Gene, as we were hurtling through space at 700 mph. But let me backtrack a bit.

My great inner awakening began with certain consciousness-expanding drugs and, not atypically, the very first of all these was pot. Although I would never consider myself a "pothead," marijuana has, on occasion, been a part of my redemption.

Back to the plane.

I was young, impetuous and immortal, and I was seated with my dear friend on a cross-country charter plane heading towards one of those once-in-a-lifetime events, the Alternative Media Conference at Goddard College where we attended meetings at night and swam naked by day.

Now, Gene was a medical doctor who found himself publishing medical advice columns and answering listeners' call-ins on FM radio, the new Town Hall for the counterculture. He became the premiere medical "Dear Abby" for the young and the toothless.

Well, we had some time on our hands as this was a cross-country flight, so Gene began opening his reader's mail. I snoozed beside him when I felt a tap on my shoulder.

"Would you like to see an interesting letter?"

"Sure, Gene."

It went something like this:

"Dear Dr. Gene: The enclosed substance fell into my hands through a neighborhood acquaintance. I have taken the liberty of rolling it into a joint with the hope you'll perform the necessary scientific research and chemical analysis. Thank you very much..."

Hmmmmm. Dr. Gene must have been reacting to a particularly fey moment. He invites me to share this extrinsic "research" by lighting a match. Well, I do recall embracing the occasion with a naughty gleam and a resounding chortle that only Lucifer could really appreciate.

Fortunately the research turned out well. The substance was benign but powerful. It stimulated the good doctor with enough brashness and playfulness that he took over the plane's entire audio system. Since this was a charter flight, the stewardess winked at Dr. Gene as he sent raucous rock'n'roll from his portable tape player through the plane's microphone, all to the utter delight of our fellow pilgrims.

Wasn't it Samuel Taylor Coleridge who opined, "He is the best physician who is the most ingenious inspirer"?

Digger
John McCleary

When you were with Digger you didn't just smoke dope, you sat upon the tripod at Delphi, partook of the blood and body of Jesus Christ, or ascended the Himalayas to commune within the cave of an ascetic.

I never knew what he was going to call his dope. "Come over and have some tea, boo, leaf, reef, greens, shit, or sacrament."

His stuff never came from Fresno; it was always Maui Wowie, Kabul Gold, Nam Green or Mendocino Mellow. Incense was as important as the lighting; music was supreme to the experience.

I never knew what he did to support his lifestyle. Style is perhaps the wrong word. His clothing was a Guatemalan shirt and nondescript faded jeans. Oh, and bare feet.

I never saw Digger outside of his place, although I have a photograph of him on his front doorstep hiding behind an album cover of Frank Zappa in front of his face with his finger in Zappa's nose.

Digger lived in a small house with two cats, one that liked the smoke of burning marijuana and one who left the premises whenever it was lit. He lived on the alley behind my house and used to call me in as I walked by.

Entering his place was like stepping into a very well-appointed dumpster or a library after the apocalypse, take your pick. The oriental rug had the patina of a pizza place. His record collection overstepped bizarre. He had cannabis buds drying in the window on a wire coat hanger.

One afternoon, I emerged from my darkroom with prints to dry on the fence. "Come on over and smoke some boo," Digger said from his kitchen window. Back into darkness, as he closed the forest green terrycloth curtains. He lit three candles and a stick of musk incense. He put on the Fugs.

It was a water pipe that day. He was using sauterne instead of water. He wore a New Year's Eve paper hat. I think I almost liked the Fugs that time.

At exactly 1:48 p.m. Digger stopped Om-ing and said he had to make a private phone call. I stumbled out. Almost back to the darkroom, I remembered my photographic tray left at Digger's. I slipped through his door and found the tray on the oriental rug. Digger, hunched over his unbelievably cluttered desk, was saying into the phone, "Sell IBM and buy that new little company named after a fruit or something."

How Do You Spell Relief?
Irwin Gooen

Unlike any number of my acquaintances back in the '60s, I had never been paranoid nor even overly concerned about smoking pot at least somewhat openly. I recall making a point of lighting up a joint when driving past the Center Street New York City Police Headquarters, and having smoked (in a regular tobacco pipe) grass on a cross-country flight, as well as on the streets of midtown Manhattan.

Eventually, when I moved to upstate New York at the end of the '60s, I smoked grass in the waiting room of a dental office, and once in the lobby of a movie house where Cheech & Chong's *Up in Smoke* was showing, and the ticket-seller scrunched her nose and remarked about the awful smell, something like rope burning. I told her that there were lotsa young people coming to see the film, and whispered that some of them were no doubt smoking pot.

Anyway, back to New York City, where one day I was driving down Flatbush Avenue in Brooklyn and smoking away in my top-down sports car. Coming the other way was a police cruiser which stopped parallel to me, and I saw the driving officer wave me over. I felt a flush in my face and thought that this was it, busted at last.

I put on the hand brake, crossed to the cruiser, and was about to say, "Hey, no—I wasn't smoking dope—just a skinny, roll-your-self cigarette," when the cop said, "Whaddaya want?"

I said, "You waved me over."

His response was, "No, we're just stopping here, and I was waving on the traffic behind us."

"Oh," I smiled. "Sorry to bother you."

Goodbye, Reno, Goodbye

My friend Bob and I went up to the Sierra skiing for a few days. He thought it would be fun to go to a show called Hello, Hollywood, Hello at the MGM Grand Hotel in Reno. It was a dinner show, $50 a plate, and when we got there we found that (a) the only thing a vegetarian could eat was canned peas, (b) we were seated with an elderly couple from Canada, and (c) the show had nothing to do with Hollywood and everything to do with breasts (except for one scene, which was aimed at the gay bondage crowd).

The show was horrid, the food worse, and my embarrassment acute, but I was well-raised and 50 bucks was a lot of money, so when Bob asked me, in the parking lot on our way back to the car, what I thought of the show, I said I'd never seen anything remotely like it, which was true.

We got into his Karmann Ghia and started back up over the mountains toward Incline Village. I wasn't saying much, and Bob decided to light up a joint. We smoked it, passing it from fingers to fingers in the light of the dashboard. It was good stuff, and presently we both had a good buzz on.

After a long silence, each with his own thoughts, I said, "God, that was good weed. It feels as if we're going five miles an hour. Wow!"

And Bob said, looking at the speedometer, "We are."

On the Border

Sometime in the '70s me and a pal were in San Francisco and we were—well, pretty stoned, actually—stuck in North Beach with no cash and low stash. So naturally we decided to hitchhike to Mexico.

We made it out to 19th Avenue and got picked up by a grungy-looking biker in a Ford van, who had just come back from Mexico and had no intention of returning. He was headed north, and picked us up assuming that we were too, since we had been thumbing a ride on the wrong side of the street.

We discussed Mexico briefly, and he let us know that he was fucking heading for Oregon, that we were fucking going with him, he would drop us off in fucking Sonoma County in time to see fucking Walt Disney with mommy and daddy, we were staying the fuck out of his stash, since it was a fucking bitch getting it across the fucking Mexican border, and by the way, we were fucking driving, since he was fucking tired.

As soon as he fell asleep, my buddy broke into his stash, and I turned the van around and headed south.

We toked and drove like maniacs, and made it to the border early the next morning. We were idling back in the line a bit, watching Governor Reagan's state troopers assist the Border Patrol by shaking down everyone under 30 who drove across from Mexico, and we were laughing and congratulating ourselves on being clever enough to be smuggling grass into Mexico, not out, when the biker woke up.

He had just slept for 12 hours in the back of a smelly van, after having been up for who-knows-how-long sweating his little score, so he probably wasn't thinking too clearly. He asked us where the fuck we were, and we told him we were at the Mexican border. He screamed like a wounded deer, grabbed the grocery bag with 14 kilos of Mexican weed, kicked open the side door of the van, and hurled it all into the brush beside the highway.

My buddy and I took one look at each other and bolted out the front doors of the van. We crossed the highway, thumbed a ride with a doughnut salesman, and got dropped off in Fresno later that day, where my aunt lived. She gave us a good meal and bus fare back to Santa Rosa.

Biker Story
Jay Lynch

Back in the days before the Summer of Love, I enjoyed smoking marijuana. I would hollow out a Winston cigarette and fill half of it with reefer. This was called a "cocktail" back then. I used to smoke these things in the school cafeteria, back when smoking was permitted in college. I figured, on the off chance that if anybody would recognize the smell, I would be down to the tobacco part of the Winston before they'd figure it was coming from my table.

When the "Legalize Pot" protests began in the early days of the hippie movement, I gave the stuff up. I didn't want to smoke pot to make a social statement. I just wanted to get high and be left alone.

Back in 1965, most people just wanted to be left alone, including a group of outlaw bikers I knew back then. True, many were dangerous psychopaths, as I look back on it all. But I must admit that as a youth I did appreciate their attitude—and I enjoyed their tales of life outside the accepted social order.

There was Deviate, who was said to have killed a mailman in Milwaukee. He wore a vest, it was told, that his old lady made for him out of the murdered postal worker's mail pouch.

There was Pony, who was able to turn into a werewolf. I had seen him undergo this metamorphosis many times. He had a wife and kid on the South Side. At home he would be a mild-mannered family man, known only by the name he was born with. But he had a separate apartment, another old lady and an outlaw identity as Pony on the North Side. It was a Jekyl and Hyde thing. In retrospect, I believe he had the power to cloud men's minds. He would arrive looking like Wally Cox. Then he'd do a werewolf take, grow a foot in stature and sprout facial hair. Eventually he got divorced. Last I heard, he was an antiques dealer in Indiana.

And then there was Reno, who chronicled it all. In the saddlebag of his Harley was his manuscript. Written in longhand on hundreds of sheets of school composition notebook paper, Reno had documented his 10 years as a member of one of the Midwest's most notorious biker gangs. He was the Kerouac of the one-percenters. Some day his book would be published. Some day his story, and the story of the fugitive culture to which he belonged, would be told. Reno was an outcast. He was a rebel. But his tattoos reflected primarily religious themes. He may have been abused and kicked around by life, but there was no question in his mind about who granted him that life. Reno believed in God!

Speed was this scribe's screwed-up drug of choice. Pot was not his scene at all. But at a biker party one night, we were all smoking reefer, including Reno. The talk was loose. Oaths, epithets and curses flowed like cheap wine. And then somebody said (I forget in what context) the words that ignited something deep within Reno's inner psyche—"God damn it! God damn it!"—the words pierced Reno's soul like a switchblade.

At first he looked flushed as he winced at the taking of the Lord's name in vain. But in seconds he turned red with some inexplicable kind of pot-induced perverse and misdirected rage.

"Yeah...God!" he snarled. "Let's talk about dear old God!"

With hate-filled eyes, Reno raised his gaze toward the ceiling. And, shaking his clenched, white-knuckled fist heavenward, he taunted his creator—daring the god, in whom he believed with every fiber of his being, to come down and take him on. Those in the crowd who knew him—and knew of his religious nature—were shocked. Here was a guy who believed in God, challenging this god to a here-and-now, kiss-my-ass fistfight. For Reno to defy God was as unbelievable as for Nixon to defy Eisenhower.

"This couldn't be happening," I thought. "This couldn't be real." But it was. His biker pals calmed him down and ushered him to a seat on the couch. Soon he chilled out. It was the reefer talking. It was the marijuana that was defying Reno's creator. It just couldn't have been Reno. Things mellowed out and the party wound down. Soon it was 4 a.m., and a group of us, including Reno, split the scene and went outside. Out on the street, we noticed that Reno's bike was missing. We heard the distant roar of the Harley's motor. Looking down the block, in the direction of the sound, we saw the shadowy silhouette of a mystery rider mounted on Reno's bike. The cycle was weaving toward us in a crazy pattern.

It was Fith, the neighborhood teenaged idiot-boy, riding up to us on Reno's cycle. We stopped him, and Reno took his Harley back. The bikers tried to intimidate the moron child, but it had no effect on Fith. That's what the other neighborhood kids called him—Fith, an acronym for "Fucked in the head."

Reno looked in his saddlebag and flipped out. His manuscript was missing. Gone was the one and only copy of the book he had so painstakingly scrawled out in ball-point, pencil, felt tip—bit by bit, day by day—over the last decade of his life. Reno grabbed the idiot-boy by the front of his Dale Evans T-shirt.

"What did you do with my papers, you little piece of shit?" he shouted.

Fith didn't register fear. He just seemed confused. "Uhhh...I trew dem in da rivah," he replied.

The sun rose that dawn, casting a pallid light on the caravan of choppers heading south toward the Chicago River bridge on Wells where it crosses to Wacker Drive. The idiot-boy was riding shotgun on the lead cycle, babbling disconcerted directions to its driver. In time we found ourselves on the bridge at the Wells Street entrance to the Merchandise Mart, staring down 50 feet or so at the count-less sheets of floating notebook paper that represented Reno's out-law life. They were irretrievable. His book would never be pub-lished.

A few months later, Reno got married to a trade journal editor. On her urging, he quit his biker gang and got a job in construc-tion.

It wasn't Reno's defiance of God that was his downfall so much as it was his belief in God. The forces that keep pot illegal likewise only have that power because we grant it to them by our belief in their authority over us. Instead of asking that marijuana be legal-ized, maybe it would just be better to just not acknowledge that the stuff is illegal—and just smoke it if you want to.

But, hey, what do I know? I have probably smoked seven or eight reefers in the last 35 years, since people found out what it was. Pot...God...I don't know.

I just want to be left alone.

Shooting Pot
Rex Weiner

My friend Chris and I were at his house one afternoon, cutting school and looking to get high. All we had was some sorry Mexican weed and no rolling papers, so he says, "Let's shoot some grass!" So we cook up some grass tea, boiling it down to a dark green liquor.

Chris gets the spoon, pulls some cotton button-backing off his shirt, and I've got the spike. I fill up the works, trying to strain this swamp mixture through the cotton, but when I hold it up to the light I can see leafy matter swimming around in there.

"What do you think?" I ask Chris.

He says, "What the hell," and bangs it into his arm.

Next it's my turn. I draw up some of the stuff and hold the works up to the light. There is a twig floating inside, but what the hell. I find the vein and shoot it in. The two of us sit around watching a stupid TV show, waiting and waiting and waiting. Nothing happens.

"I'm going home," I say. "My mom's cooking something special for dinner and I don't want to get in trouble."

Later I'm sitting at the table with my dad, my little brother and my mom, eating beef stroganoff, when I feel the blood drain out of my face and my stomach turning violent flip-flops.

"What's the matter?" my mom asks. "Don't you like the beef stroganoff? I made it especially for you."

My shithead brother, knowing I hate the food, says, "Hey, how come your face is green?"

I said that the food was great, I was just feeling a little sick from something I ate at school. I went to my room and was in bad shape for several days. Must have been that twig got stuck in my aorta. In any case, my mom never made beef stroganoff again.

Chapter 24

Roaches

But Who's Counting?
Kit Sibert

As for pot stories, well, I got really paranoid once. And another time I couldn't stop laughing and thought that was like *Hell*. And another time I got jumpy legs and had to put them straight out in front of me (I was sitting down) for about 100 hours. And about 534 times I had to eat everything in the refrigerator. And about 342 times I got totally tired and went to sleep. And once I acted really stupid. I didn't cotton to pot much. Is that what you had in mind?

Problem Child

I'm a child-and-adolescent psychiatrist, and one day in the early 1980s these two parents drag their 14-year-old delinquent into the office so I can treat his "dope" problem.

Their explanation was, "We don't care if he smokes pot, but you have to get him to stop copping *ours*."

Actual Dialogue
Wildman Weiner

"So, I'm over at Carole's..."
    "Carole?"
    "In Brentwood."
    "I think I know her."
    "I don't think you know her. I don't think I know her. I don't
think she knows herself."
    "Whattaya mean?"
    "She's sitting on her couch weeping."
        *   *   *
    "That's a nice fabric, Carole," I say.
    "It should be," she barks. "It cost a mint!"
    "Oh," I say. She returns to her weeping. "What's wrong?" I ask,
and she sniffles.
    "Everyone's always coming over here to get high and hang out
all day and night and I can never get rid of them and I just want to
be left alone! I've got so much to do!"
    "Why don't you just throw them out?"
    "I can't," she wails. "*I'm* the dealer!"

The Hole
Hal Muskat

There was that time I took a cube of hash off the serving tray in an Algerian cafe (down one alley, turn left at another alley, take a right and another right into yet another, smaller alley) and, as was the custom, brought it into the WC where, alone in the dark with the hole in the middle of the floor, I somehow found my chillum and got so stoned that I couldn't find my way out the door. I mean I couldn't find the door. The hole was the center of the universe. There was no out. Fuckin' joint stunk from colonial Algerian and hippie shit.

Moment of Truth

Four smugglers are sitting around a freezing apartment in Srinagar
(imagine a place that adult human-size rabbits built, a warren
three stories tall, hundreds of years old, no right angles), waiting
for the best of the best to waft its way down from the Hindu Kush.
They have been waiting for three months.

Whenever they ask their main man, Rashid, what's the status, he
looks out the window, up and down the street, as if the shipment
were just about at the front door. He turns to the gringos and says
it's no problem. How reassuring. Business in Kashmiriville.

Smoking 10 joints a day or so of the world's best hash, joints as
thick as your forefinger, and now, now, they are running out of
stash. The unthinkable. As the last joint is rolled, they all give each
other a sly look, reach into various nooks and crannies, and come
out with a kilo apiece that each, thinking he is the only sane one
of the bunch, the only one with foresight, had squirreled away.

Suddenly there are 10 pounds of hash on the floor.

Brownie Baked

This has happened to three different parents. My friends leave brownies in the fridge and, not knowing they are loaded, their dad eats one or more. All three times the dad has sat down in front of the TV and laughs and smiles a lot more than usual. Two of the three dads then stayed up later than usual and fell asleep in their La-Z-Boy (not a normal thing for them to do). The next morning they all said that they slept great, and wanted more brownies.

Choices
Eric Furry

When my friend Whitey and I first started smoking pot, he went into the drugstore and asked for a pack of rolling papers.

"Gummed or ungummed?" the clerk asked.

"Ungummed," Whitey replied quickly, not wanting to appear foolish.

Predictably, he was chastised when he returned home.

"Next time just ask for a pack of Zig-Zags," a roommate remarked.

Needless to say, that's exactly what he did the next time.

"Wheat or rice?" asked the clerk.

"Gummed," Whitey responded.

Then there's the story of my stoned girlfriend being asked for her visa at Amsterdam's Centraal Station, to which she replied, "I don't have a Visa—is MasterCard okay?"

Light Show

One evening after some relatively intense smoking, three friends of mine were out cruising when they happened to be pulled over by the Man. After checking the driver's ID, the cop shined his flashlight in the face of the very stoned person in the back seat, whose response was, "Strobe it, officer."

Evangelism
Dan Newman

While hitchhiking in Oregon, I goofed and left my fanny-pack on the side of the road. It contained the usuals—including my wallet and my dope.

Two weeks later I received the fanny-pack in the mail. Everything was returned, including the money, except for the dope.

The good Samaritan had replaced the pot with religious pamphlets.

Time Delay
A.J. Pirilli

When I first came to Japan, I shared a rented house with six other people. One evening, while cruising the richer neighborhoods for usable trash—which is a popular pastime of foreigners in Japan on the night before the heavy trash is to be collected—I found a shortwave radio.

When I took it home and tried it out, I realized that it needed some sort of an antenna. While I was taking the steel strings off my guitar to fashion them into an outside antenna, one of my housemates came into my room with a friend of his who had just arrived from a Southeast Asian nation with a rather large lump of hashish concealed in his undershorts.

It was agreed that the three of us would try it out as I tried out my new radio, once the antenna was in place. He made his preparations and I made mine.

"I have no idea how good this stuff is," he said.

"Well, we'll soon find out," I answered back as I switched on the shortwave.

We puffed a bit and I fiddled with the dials, and suddenly we could hear a clear voice in English:

"...and...that...is...the...cur...rent...sit...ua...tion...on...Wall..."

I choked up some smoke to say, "Wow, this is some really good shit. Talk about gettin' spaced."

The three of us sat there, grinning and chuckling over our good fortune.

Then the man on the radio:

"This...has...been...the...world...news...spoken...in...slow...English... for...foreign...listeners."

Paradigm Shift
Jonathan Pekar

My brother Jefferson and his friend Steve are hanging out in a Volkswagen bus—they had searched the whole car for roaches—when the cops come up.

"What are you all doing?"

"We're just sitting here getting ready to drink beer. We haven't started yet."

"You guys don't have any pot in here, do you?"

"No, sir, there ain't no pot in this car."

"Lemme look in the back too."

And he opens it up and closes it up real quick.

"That's cool," the cop says. "I like your van. Now don't be drinking and driving—you guys should be smoking instead of drinking."

That's weird. The cops drive off. My brother and his friend sit there for a minute, and then they drive home. My brother goes in the car, opens up the back, and fuckin' laying there is a film can which the cops left there, a half ounce of Chronic marijuana.

"Well, dude," my brother says, "we searched the car for an hour. It's an empty van. There were no roaches, nothing in the whole car, then I open up the back and it's laying there. You gonna tell me two guys looking for an hour can't find it? A film canister? There's no way. Dude, look at this Chronic!"

It was purple, I mean purple, and the cops put it there. It was a gift—"You guys should be smoking instead of drinking"—and they left. I'll never forget my brother coming in: "Dude, you'll never believe this, ever." I grilled him for hours. I said, "This didn't happen." He says, "No, come look, it was an empty van." Those cops must have had a good laugh, can you imagine? Perverse, but good perverse.

It almost seems like the cops have lightened up. They don't care if you're smoking it, they just don't want you selling. It's all about, "Don't be a drug dealer." But when it gets to the point where cops are giving you pot, is that just not the fuckin' weirdest thing you ever heard? I could not get over how wacky that was.